TAHQUITZ AND SUICIDE ROCKS

AMERICAN ALPINE CLUB
CLIMBER'S GUIDE

TAHQUITZ
AND
SUICIDE
ROCKS

Edited by
CHUCK WILTS

THE ALPINE AMERICAN CLUB

NEW YORK

Sixth Edition, 1979
ISBN 0–930410–07–6
Library of Congress Catalog Card Number 79-87634

Printed in the United States of America

Frontispiece
Tahquitz Rock from the Northwest
Photo by B. Turney

A climber's guide
is no substitute for
skill and experience.

In the ultimate analysis,
good judgment is the
essential ingredient of
safe climbing.

PREFACE

This may be the last edition of the *Tahquitz and Suicide Guide*. Even the climbers of the present generation seem to agree that the basic purpose of the guide has been fulfilled and that there is no real need to record more and more difficult variations of existing routes. The purpose of this editor's final edition is primarily to bring the material in the supplements and a few new routes into proper order in the text. At the same time this provides a last opportunity to delete or rewrite outdated material. For historical perspective, some material from the prefaces of earlier editions is included below.

Technical climbing on Tahquitz Rock began in 1936 when the new Southern Chapter Rock Climbing Section of the Sierra Club established four climbing routes on the west side of the rock. For nearly seven years, the routes were passed on by word of mouth, although there is a cryptic remark in a 1938 Sierra Club Bulletin that a guide had been written for the six known routes. If such a guide existed, no copies have survived. By 1943, the number of routes had increased to fourteen and Bill Shand published what is considered the first edition—a half-dozen mimeographed pages. For another decade this proved adequate since active search for new routes was not begun until the early 1950s when a new generation of climbers established new levels of proficiency and technique. These climbers discovered more than thirty new routes in a period of a few years.

The second edition of the guide book, written by Don Wilson and Chuck Wilts in 1956, described forty-seven routes under a new grading system. In the third edition of 1962, many route descriptions were rewritten and twenty more routes were inserted. The fourth edition of 1970 was used to add twenty new routes at Tahquitz, but its main purpose was to include in a single volume, guides to the two companion formations: Tahquitz and Suicide Rocks. The original task of collecting the detailed route descriptions for Suicide Rock had been ably accomplished by Pat Callis and Charlie Raymond. They generously acceded to the suggestion that the two guides be published as one volume. Following publication of that edition, Suicide became an instant success. Within three years the number of routes at Suicide doubled, hence the fifth edition in 1973.

It is not possible to give individual credit to all the climbers who have helped compile this guide, but their assistance has been appreciated. I apologize for those cases where I have been unable to accurately describe their achievements on the printed page. Excellent photographs have been provided by several climbers, particularly Larry Reynolds and Burt Turney.

Chuck Wilts
Pasadena, 1979

CONTENTS

TAHQUITZ AND SUICIDE ROCKS

INTRODUCTION

Lily Rock, or Tahquitz Rock as it is known to climbers in Southern California, is an attractive dome shaped formation on the west side of Tahquitz Peak in the San Jacinto Mountains. It is composed of massive granitic rock similar to that found in the Sierra Nevada, and has a summit elevation of about 8000 feet. Suicide Rock is a smaller rocky outcrop directly across Strawberry Valley from Tahquitz Rock. Its summit is about 500 feet lower. Together they have developed into the major rock climbing area of Southern California because of the excellent quality of the rock, the wide range of climbing difficulty, the high exposure, and because of easy accessibility and mild climate.

Most of the routes on Tahquitz are found on rock faces with very little chimney or ridge climbing. The routes extend in height to almost 1000 feet and range in difficulty from easy scrambling to very difficult direct aid climbing. Suicide Rock is much smaller than Tahquitz, but it offers a surprisingly broad spectrum of climbing. There are routes up massive blank faces which utilize delicate friction at one extreme, and challenging jam cracks and flaring chimneys at the other. Most of the routes are short—only one to three pitches in length. But they make up for this in difficulty since more than half are rated 5.9 and above in difficulty. The two areas combined offer more than 200 climbing routes to challenge the abilities of both novice and expert climbers.

HISTORY OF
TAHQUITZ AND SUICIDE ROCKS

Tahquitz Rock is the most striking landmark in the San Jacinto Mountains. In the years before the white man, the Indians found it an intriguing natural phenomenon and embedded it deeply into their religious beliefs. Some sixty-six years ago, Phebe Spalding summarized the then current legends as follows.

"The Indians aver that this rock covers the doorway of the deep cave in which Tahquitch (the Indian equivalent of Devil) dwells. Thither in misty legend was borne centuries ago an Indian maiden of a tribe now unknown; and to her unwilling company were added later, other beautiful maidens whom Tahquitch from time to time captured from neighboring tribes.

"A curious rumbling of the mountain occurs in certain of the summer months; and the Indians believe that this phenomenon is caused by the violent anger of Tahquitch when his quest for a new bride is unsuccessful, or by the restlessness of his cave-imprisoned victims."

There are other forms of the legend, differing in detail and substance, but in all of them, Tahquitz Rock covers the lair of a devil, not a very propitious omen for a rock destined to become a great rock climbing center.

14

The deep rumbling sound heard in the valley is not just legend according to the present residents of Idyllwild. In recent years the local newspaper, *The Town Crier,* featured a series of articles covering all aspects of the phenomenon from the ancient Indian legends to recent investigations seeking to uncover a natural cause. The most plausible hypothesis found has been an unusual atmospheric condition giving rise to a particular wind pattern through the rocky ridges above the valley, but the mystery has not really been solved. Climbers unravelling a delicate 5.10 or 5.11 route will find occasional sonic booms from March Field or El Toro aircraft much more of a mental hazard than the gentle rumbling of the mountains.

The summit of Tahquitz Rock was a well known goal of the mountain hiker in the early 1900s, but technical climbing was unknown until the formation of the Rock Climbing Section of the Sierra Club. In 1936, the rock was first noted as a potential climbing area by Jim Smith and Mary Jane Edwards as they hiked past it on a descent from Tahquitz Peak. That same year, Jim returned with four other members of the Rock Climbing Section, and they pioneered four routes on the west side of the rock. The growth of new routes was at first sporadic; only twelve were known in 1943, but by 1960 the number had mushroomed to sixty. Today (1979), Tahquitz Rock is recognized as the finest climbing area in Southern California, with over ninety routes to challenge the abilities of both novice and expert climbers.

Suicide Rock, being much smaller, attracted little attention before the dawn of technical rock climbing. The name also appears to come from early Indian legends, but they are not as well authenticated as the Tahquitz story. The development of Suicide Rock as a climbing area began in 1966. Two routes were found in an early exploratory trip before 1950, but Tahquitz had just entered its golden era of expansion and the general consensus was that Tahquitz presented greater and more interesting challenges. The real potential of Suicide Rock was first recognized by Pat Callis and Charlie Raymond. Between 1966 and 1968 they pioneered about thirty routes and presented their findings to the climbing community in the 1970 edition of this guide. Since that time the rock has continued to gain in popularity and draws climbing crowds that sometimes exceed those at Tahquitz. Today (1979), Suicide Rock has well over one hundred recognized routes.

Unlike most climbing areas, the climbing history at Tahquitz and Suicide Rocks was unmarred by serious accident for twenty-three years. During this period, two noteworthy incidents ended happily. In 1950, Joe Fitschen was descending the rock by way of the Friction Route—unroped of course since this is an easy 3rd class route of descent. Getting off route at the top, he attempted a difficult delicate traverse, slipped and fell about 170 feet thereby discovering a new route (See Route 78). Although badly battered, Joe miraculously was not permanently injured. To the amazement of all, he was climbing at Tahquitz again within a few months.

In the second incident which happened about the same time, Fred Martin gave a dynamic demonstration on the Sahara Terror that one could fall eighty feet on nylon rope and suffer far less damage than the belayer.

In 1959, the first climbing fatality occurred at Tahquitz. A rock dislodged by a climber near the top of the rock resulted in the death of a young French climber who thought

16

he was crouched safely at the base of the rock. Other fatal or serious accidents have continued at an accelerating rate up to the present time, many of them reported in some detail in earlier editions of the guide. In almost every case, carelessness or bad judgement was a major contributing factor. This is not meant to imply that rock climbing is free of hazards, but at least to repeat that with care the hazards can be greatly reduced.

GEOLOGICAL HISTORY OF THE TAHQUITZ AREA

Some hundred million years ago, the land area of Southern and Baja California was intruded from below by plutonic rock forming a batholith of unusual size. Now called the Southern California batholith, it extends roughly from Riverside to the southern tip of Baja California, a length of about one thousand miles. In Southern California it has a width of some fifty or sixty miles and forms the principal rock of the mountain ranges south of the Los Angeles basin between Imperial Valley and the ocean. Although not as spectacular as the great batholith of the Sierra Nevada it is actually somewhat larger.

For many years it was supposed that the Sierra Nevada batholith was intruded in late Jurassic time and the Southern California batholith in mid to late Cretaceous time. This would make the rock of the Sierra considerably older. Recently geologists have obtained more accurate estimates of the age of these rocks by a study of the slight radioactivity or radioactive end-products of naturally occurring minerals such as zircons in the granitic rocks. These estimates have been very close to one hundred million years in both bath-

17

oliths, placing them both in middle Cretaceous time. (In reference to animal life on earth, this represents the climax of dinosaur life. Soon after this period they died out and the development of mammals began.)

As the batholith was uplifted, the surface rock was largely eroded away and the batholith was fractured by several large parallel faults trending from north-northwest to south-southeast. One of the greatest of these is the San Jacinto fault which forms the west and southwest boundaries of the San Jacinto Mountains. These mountains are also bounded on the north and east by lesser fault-zones. The San Jacinto Mountains were uplifted through these three zones in a large triangular block eight to ten thousand feet above the surrounding terrain. The presence of large prominent benches at eight to nine thousand feet on the east side (Tahquitz Valley and Round Valley) and at an altitude of 5500 feet on the west side suggest the uplift may have occurred in at least three widely separated periods, with the benches being the result of stream planation before the next uplift occurred. In a certain sense the last period may still be active since the San Jacinto fault at the western base of the mountains is one of the active major faults in Southern California. In the period 1780–1928, ninety-two earthquakes were attributed to this fault-zone— six times more than any other. There were two violent earthquakes in 1899 and 1918, each of which practically destroyed the towns of San Jacinto and Hemet. Both of these probably originated on this fault. In the last fifty years, activity at least in the form of large earthquakes appears to have diminished.

Strictly speaking, Tahquitz Rock is not granite. Most of the San Jacinto Mountains, in fact most of the exposed Southern California batholith, consists of a medium grained quartz diorite called tonalite. This rock differs from true granite in the proportion of crystalline constituents. It is higher in calcium, iron and magnesium minerals, and relatively deficient in potassium and silica. In terms of constituent minerals, the feldspar is almost entirely andesine (calcium-rich plagioclase) with very little orthoclase (the potassium feldspar). It is also relatively rich in the dark minerals hornblende and biotite. The only other mineral of consequence is quartz. Other minerals are present in minute amounts, e.g., the zircons which have been used to give a radioactive date or age to the rock. It is presumed that

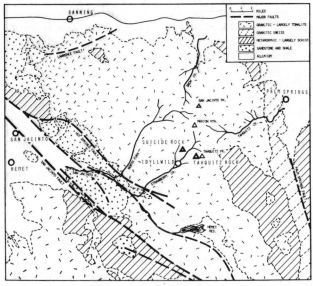

GEOLOGIC MAP OF SAN JACINTO MOUNTAINS

Tahquitz Rock is tonalite although it does not appear to have been specifically examined.

LOCATION OF TAHQUITZ ROCK

Tahquitz Rock is located near the mountain resort village of Idyllwild which is easily reached from the Los Angeles area by way of Riverside or Redlands. The simplest route follows Interstate Highway 15 southeast from Riverside to a point just beyond Perris where State Highway 74 branches left to Hemet and on into the southern part of the San Jacinto Mountains. A well-marked side road leads left to Idyllwild. Another route preferred by some climbers follows Interstate 10 beyond Redlands to Banning. Here signs point off the freeway to a mountain road that runs southeastward to Idyllwild. Several other routes can be found by an enterprising driver and may be preferred because of shortness, or merely for variety.

There are several campgrounds near Idyllwild. The ones used most often by climbers are the Riverside County public campground which is entered by following signs to the left as one enters Idyllwild, or the State Park which is just past the center of town on the road leading to Banning. There is a fee for use of either campground. There are also lodges, grocery stores and restaurants in the village. The driving distance from Los Angeles is about 130 miles.

Tahquitz Rock is about two miles east-northeast of Idyllwild. On the USGS topographic map (Palm Springs quadrangle) it is named Lily Rock. It can be seen readily from Idyllwild, with Tahquitz Peak (8828 feet) above and to the right, and Marion Mountain (10,332 feet) on the left. The principal road into Fern Valley is the Fern Valley Road which runs northeastward from Circle Drive. Near the end of Fern Valley Road, a short road branches to the left and in one half mile ends at a large parking area, Humber Park, where the Mt. San Jacinto trail begins. Water is available at this area except during unusually dry years or in winter when the pipes are drained to prevent damage from freezing.

Just below the parking area a prominent bridle trail runs southeast passing directly below Tahquitz Rock. About a quarter mile from the parking area a narrow steep trail branches to the left leading directly to the rock. The trail zigzags up the steep hillside keeping just to the right of the prominent rockslide extending down from the center of the rock. At the head of the trail is Lunch Rock, a popular meeting place for both climbers and spectators. This large boulder or group of boulders lies just below the West Face on which nearly half of the climbing routes are found. Total time for the hike to Lunch Rock is about thirty or forty minutes. Descent requires only fifteen or twenty minutes. Due to the large number of persons passing Lunch Rock, it is unwise to leave valuable equipment untended.

LOCATION OF SUICIDE ROCK

Suicide Rock is located directly across Strawberry Valley from Tahquitz Rock. It is two miles north of the town of Idyllwild, and about one mile northwest of Tahquitz Rock. Suicide Rock is usually approached from a sharp right turn in the road less than one-half mile below Humber Park. This point is well-marked by a pair of large water storage tanks. The terrain leading to the rock is almost uniformly free of underbrush and talus so that many approach routes

21

are possible. However one particularly good trail has developed and climbers are urged to use it to minimize damage to the surrounding terrain. The trail reaches the rock at the base of the East Buttress, the lowest point on the rock. The hike to Suicide Rock requires about twenty minutes.

CLASSIFICATION OF ROUTES

The rating of climbing routes has always been a problem and is now even more controversial. Not only are a myriad of systems available, but there are those who argue that the rating and even the route description inevitably detract from the climbing experience. Nevertheless, ratings are inevitable wherever climbers congregate in large numbers, and certainly that is the case at Tahquitz and Suicide Rocks. For an area like this, two important features of a rating system are simplicity, so that it is easy to use, and that it be open ended so that expansion is possible as climbing skills evolve.

An attempt at worldwide standardization was made in 1968 when a new international UIAA system for grading climbs was approved both unanimously and unenthusiastically by the delegates from the twenty-three member countries at the annual assembly of the UIAA (Union Internationale des Associations d'Alpinisme). If any international system is to be successful, it is probably the UIAA system, but after ten years, the experiment seems a failure, at least in the United States.

The Tahquitz decimal system dates back well over twenty years, and now that climbers recognize it as an open-ended system that does not stop at 5.9, it serves the purpose as well as any other. It is worth noting that through the years the maximum rating of free ascents at Tahquitz and Suicide has risen from 5.9 through 5.10 and 5.11, and now stands at 5.12. It is also an unassailable fact that most climbing here is done by climbers who are intimately familiar with this system and generally unfamiliar with the UIAA. The decimal system is therefore continued in this edition of the guide. For purposes of comparison, the UIAA classifications are correlated with this system in the list of standards that ends this section. If a climber is accustomed to still other standards, he will simply have to make a few ascents to get the calibration needed if he wishes to use this feature of the guide.

The decimal system is used to subdivide the 5th class climbing routes. These are routes in which ropes and chocks or pitons are used for protection by most climbers. The decimal number indicates the technical difficulty of the most difficult pitch (more accurately the most difficult move) on a particular route. An easy 5th class route will be rated 5.0 or 5.1 while a route of exceptional severity (i.e., clearly impossible) will currently be rated 5.12. Many expert climbers feel that there was too great a delay in setting up the 5.11 standard and that 5.10 covers too great a range of difficulty. Some of them have subdivided 5.10 into four categories both here and in Yosemite. Although I understand their concern, I do not see the real need for such a fine gradation in this guide. Instead I have chosen to use 5.10 and 5.10+ as two distinct levels in this edition, the first including both 5.10A and B, and the second covering 5.10C and D.

Direct aid routes have been subdivided into four classifications—easy, moderate, difficult, and very difficult—indicated by the designation A1 to A4 respectively. None of the Tahquitz or Suicide routes seem to rate the A5 classification used on the most difficult Yosemite routes. In earlier editions of the guide, about twenty-six routes were listed as aid routes, offering a complete range in direct aid climbing difficulty. With only a few exceptions, these routes have now been climbed free, in some cases requiring extraordinary effort and gaining new classifications of 5.11 and 5.12. The dilemma presented is that by some ethical standards these routes are no longer available as aid routes. However, the intermediate (or expert) climber not capable of 5.11 or 5.12 moves may still find these routes useful for aid practice. For this reason, both classifications are given for the major routes of this group.

In addition to an index of difficulty, the length of the routes on Tahquitz Rock is indicated by giving a "typical time of ascent." This is a rough measure of the climbing time for a two-man party of good but not exceptional ability.

In each edition, route classifications are kept as current as possible, but changes do occur either abruptly when handholds pull off, or more gradually as the shoes of hundreds of climbers gradually polish critical footholds. If you find errors or changes in the ratings be sure to publicize them within the climbing community.

WHITE FIR
Abies concolor

ROUTE STANDARDS AT TAHQUITZ AND SUICIDE ROCKS

Decimal	Name	UIAA

Free Roped Climbing

Decimal	Name	UIAA
5.0	The Trough	III
5.1	White Maiden's Walkaway	III+
5.2	Frightful Variation of the Trough	IV−
5.3	East Lark	IV
5.4	Angel's Fright	IV+
5.5	Ski Tracks	V−
5.6	Sahara Terror	V
5.7	Fingertrip	V+
5.8	Mechanic's Route	VI−
5.9	Open Book	VI
5.10	Blank	VI+
5.11	Valhalla	
5.12	The Hangover	

Direct Aid Climbing

A1	The Reach	A1
A2	Lower Royal's Arch	A2
A3	The Hangover	A3
A4	The Vampire	A4

All of the direct aid standards have been climbed free but are very difficult without aid. The direct aid rating will be valid for those climbers unable to climb 5.11 or 5.12 pitches.

MISCELLANY

ROUTE DESCRIPTIONS

In describing routes, an attempt has been made to strike a reasonable balance between descriptions which are painfully detailed and those which are so sketchy as to be useless. It is hoped that the climber using this guide will never be led astray, nor will he have any of the delightful climbing problems solved for him. When directions right or left are used in a route description they refer to the right or left side of a person facing into the rock. Most of the terms used in descriptions are familiar to all climbers with perhaps one exception. A particularly common crack at Tahquitz is one formed by the intersection of two faces of rock. In many cases they intersect at nearly a right angle (Routes 13 and 54), in other cases at an obtuse angle (Route 21). In either case the term dihedral is used to describe such a crack, although strictly speaking the word dihedral should apply to the geometric figure formed by two intersecting planes and not just to the line of intersection.

TREES

There are many trees which are particularly useful in locating and describing routes at Tahquitz Rock. Most of these are conifers. It is assumed that most climbers can differentiate these trees on sight or at least by casual inspection. The most common are:

1. White Fir (*abies concolor*) Short single needles.

2. Yellow Pines (*pinus jeffreyi* and *coulteri*) Long six inch needles, three to a bundle.

3. Sugar or White Pine (*pinus lambertiana*) Medium three inch needles, five to a bundle.

4. Mountain Mahogany (*cercocarpus ledifolius*) Grey furrowed bark, leaves lanceolate one inch long and one quarter inch wide. Typically grows as a shrub tree.

Oaks are less common, and specific varieties have not been identified. Not particularly useful in locating routes, but still noteworthy are some beautiful azaleas *(rhododendron occidentale)* found at the base of the rock on the north side. They are usually in bloom in May or June.

CLIMBING EQUIPMENT

It is probably unnecessary to remark that ropes are regarded as necessary for most of the routes at Tahquitz and Suicide Rocks. A single 11 mm perlon or nylon rope 120 feet long is satisfactory for most of the routes. However, most climbers prefer to use 150- or 165-foot ropes.

As a matter of policy, climbers are urged to use chocks or nuts both for protection and aid wherever possible and to use pitons only where absolutely necessary. On popular climbs it is particularly urged that the necessary pitons be left in place as fixed pins, and that climbers no longer try to leave the routes clean. This is a complete reversal from the plea for clean routes in earlier editions of the guide. The great surge of climbing activity in the last ten years, the tendency of beginners to overdrive pitons, and the perfection of the alloy steel piton—particularly the angle—have resulted in unfortunate damage to the piton cracks on popular routes.

The chocks and nuts used most frequently range from ⅛ to 2 inches in size. Although each climber has individual preferences, #3 to #6 stoppers are probably used with greatest frequency. Expansion anchors have been used on about one-third of the routes on Tahquitz and over half of the routes at Suicide. These are permanent anchors which require no special fittings and they will accept ordinary carabiners. By convention these anchors are usually called expansion bolts or simply bolts, although this is strictly speaking a misnomer for the types in common use.

Most of the routes at Tahquitz and Suicide can be protected entirely with chocks, expansion bolts and fixed pitons. However, some of the more difficult routes (e.g., The Flakes) do not seem to retain the necessary fixed pins, and some difficult aid routes (e.g., The X-crack) are not easily done without pitons or rather specialized direct-aid gear.

RESCUE

Because of the large number of climbs made at Tahquitz and Suicide, the probability of an accident, while small, is very real. For this reason, two Stokes litters have been cached at Tahquitz and one at Suicide. At Tahquitz, one litter is located at the top of the first pitch of the Angel's Fright on a ledge appropriately called Litter Ledge. The other is lashed to a tree at the bottom of the South Face near the Orange Peel. At Suicide Rock, the litter is lashed to a tree at the bottom of the Weeping Wall (East Face). Anyone using one of the litters should be honor bound to see that it is replaced promptly.

WINTER CLIMBING

Winter ascents at Tahquitz may require additional equipment—an ice axe or ice hammer, mittens, proper footgear. More protection may be required and most 5th class climbs become aid climbs if much ice is found on the rock. Ice usually persists on the north side from December to March although one sunny day will remove most of it from the south side. Snow and ice avalanches have been experienced in gullies such as the Trough. They are generally limited in extent, but are not particularly pleasant even when small.

RAPPELLING

When rappelling for pleasure, trees or expansion bolts are usually used to establish rappel points. In most cases the rope may be placed directly around a tree if care is taken to lay it in such a way that it will not jam. At Tahquitz, the most popular rappel route is just right of the Angel's Fright. Trees may be used to establish all four rappel points, and the rappel ends just above Lunch Rock. Some of the commonly used rappel routes at Suicide are described in the text of the guide.

PERMITS

Since Tahquitz Rock is located in a Wilderness Area, an entry permit is required for each person or party entering the area. The U.S. Forest Service Administration hopes their procedure will be simple enough so that climbers will not be unduly inconvenienced. Those not familiar with the permit procedure should inquire (in person, by mail, or telephone) at the Idyllwild Ranger Station located at 25925 Village Center Drive, Idyllwild, California. Mailing address: P.O. Box 518, Idyllwild CA 92349. Telephone: 714–659–2117.

ARRANGEMENT OF THE GUIDE

Tahquitz

The routes are given in geographical order, starting at the Notches to the east and progressing around the rock in a counterclockwise direction. For convenience of the user, the routes are divided into natural groups, and the area containing each group is described first. The area descriptions will therefore be found in the main text of the guide preceding the routes of that area. If a particular route is sought, it often can be located more quickly by first referring to the area description. Nearly all of the routes may be found in the photographs of the north, west and south sides of the rock. Two photographs are provided for each side. In one of the pair, the most prominent routes have been sketched in with dotted lines and have been labeled The photographs are particularly useful for locating and identifying routes on the north side. All routes are listed alphabetically in the index along with the rating of technical difficulty.

Suicide

Suicide Rock, though smaller than Tahquitz Rock, is a more complex structure. As a result, the natural geographic regions cannot be ordered in a simple counterclockwise pattern. In the text of the guide, each area is described with its relation to the other regions, and this is followed by the route descriptions of that region. The geographical units are given in the following order: Southern Region, the Smooth Soul Wall, the Sunshine (SE) Face, East Buttress, the Weeping Wall (E Face), Northern Area. Within each unit, the routes are numbered and listed in sequence from left to right (south to north). The routes are listed alphabetically in the index along with the rating of technical difficulty.

THE CLIMBING ROUTES
ON
TAHQUITZ ROCK

TAHQUITZ ROCK

ROUTE 1

1. SUMMIT VIA THE NOTCHES

a. SOUTHWEST ROUTE   Class 2

The Notches form the gap where Tahquitz Rock joins the ridge leading to Tahquitz Peak. From the southwest the Notches are easily reached by game trails up the scree in the draw on the south side of the rock. From the Notches it is an easy scramble to the summit along the south side of the ridge.

b. NORTHEAST ROUTE   Class 3

Circle left under the North face of the rock on easy talus.

Gullies lead directly to the Notches from the northeast side of the rock. The class 3 pitches are just below the Notches. Continue to summit as in Route 1a.

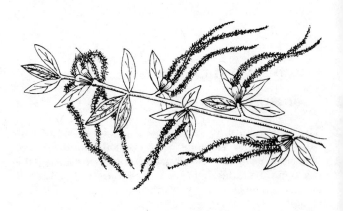

MOUNTAIN MAHOGANY
Cercocarpus ledifolius

THE NORTHEAST FACE

ROUTES 2–8

The Northeast Face extends from the Northeast Rib near the Notches on the left to the North Buttress on the right. The Northeast Rib is well defined and unmistakable. However, the North Buttress is rather poorly defined, consisting of a shallow projection on the north side of the rock. In the photograph of the North Face, the buttress is near the center of the picture, bounded on the left by a wide shadow extending to the top of the rock. The North Buttress can be readily identified since the base of the rock dips sharply on approaching from the right, and then extends nearly horizontally to the chutes near the Northeast Rib. The bottom of the Northeast Face is the lowest region of the rock.

At least two ascents of the North and Northeast Faces were made in the late 1930s and reported in Shand's original guide. The descriptions are of little use in locating the routes although there is a vague resemblance to the routes now known as the Lark and the North Buttress. There are about six main lines of ascent now recognized on the North-east Face, and a number of very interesting variations.

A short distance to the right of the Northeast Rib, two scree gullies lead up and left toward the rib. The first one becomes a rock chimney offering an interesting yet easy 5th class approach to the Northeast Rib. The one on the right is the longer of the two and is readily identified by a very large sugar pine growing at the mouth of the gully. The scree in the gully extends up some 50 feet and is followed by one or two hundred feet of 3rd class scrambling. At this point an easy 4th class broken chimney leads diagonally left to the Northeast Rib. At the same point, the Northeast Farce (Route 3) leads up the face to the right, bordered on the left by a small buttress or dihedral. This dihedral is well marked in the photograph of the north side by a long black shadow one-half inch from the left margin. About 100 feet down the gully, the great overhang of El Grandote (Route 4) can be seen about 30 feet up the right wall of the gully. At the mouth of the gully and just above the sugar pine mentioned earlier, a prominent crack leads straight up the rock. This is the start of the east variation of the Northeast Face (Route 5).

About 50 yards to the right of this point, exfoliation slabs have been cut by a vertical joint in the rock. Slabs to the right have fallen away to a depth of four to six feet, leaving a shallow right angle wall of this height on the left which runs in a remarkably straight line more than half way up the rock. In the photograph of the north face this wall shows up as a discontinuous bright sunlit streak in the middle of the Northeast Face. The standard Northeast Face Route follows the right angle dihedral formed by this wall and the steep face of rock to the right.

Farther right about 200 feet just at the edge of the

North Buttress is another right angle recess formed by the same face of rock on the left and the North Buttress on the right. This is the starting point for the Lark (Route 7) and its variations. The North Buttress is a split buttress at the bottom. The Uneventful (Route 8) and its Hubris variation ascend the left branch of the buttress.

2. NORTHEAST RIB   Class 5.0   2 hours

FA: October 1940; J. & R. Mendenhall

Several routes have been used on the Northeast Rib which range from class 4 to easy class 5 in difficulty. Detailed route description is unnecessary. The buttress of the rib can be approached from the left, that is from the very bottom of the rib, or from either of two small gullies which lead up to the rib from the right. Climb on or slightly left of the crest for the easiest climbing. A more interesting route is found if the climber stays on the right side of the rib. One or two chocks is enough for most variations.

3. NORTHEAST FARCE   Class 5.4   3 hours

FA: September 1954; D. Wilson, J. Gallwas

The beginning of this route is given in detail in the description of the North Face routes. At the upper end of the second (right) gully, climbing begins in the dihedral between the face on the right and the buttress of the Northeast Rib. Ascend 50 or 60 feet and make a delicate traverse 30 feet right to a deep wide crack on the face. Continue up for about three pitches to the left edge of some overhangs that extend up and right all the way over to the Lark (Route 7).

Climb over the overhang at the easiest spot and continue on 3rd or 4th class climbing to the top of the Northeast Rib. Several climbers have complained that the traverse is much more difficult than the original rating of 5.3. Perhaps the present rating will satisfy them, though I insist the problem is psychological, not technical. Five or six chocks will be used; include some large ones.

VARIATION 1

Three pitches above the traverse, the regular route crosses near the left edge of some overhangs that extend right and up all the way over to the Lark. An easy but very interesting traverse under these overhangs can be used to connect with the upper pitches of the Northeast Face (Route 5) or the Lark (Route 7). (C. & E. Wilts)

VARIATION 2

The dihedral in which the route begins can be ascended for about 200 feet to a point where an overhang blocks easy progress. Steep broken rock leads to the left where the route joins the Northeast Rib. (G. Harr)

VARIATION 3—EL WHAMPO   Class 5.7

El Whampo takes a much more direct line; the Farce first ascends to its left, then traverses to its right, and finally near the top crosses again to the left. Start about 30 feet right of the dihedral which marks the start of the Farce. Ascend a mossy crack a short distance and traverse left about 20 feet to a series of small overhangs about ten feet from the Farce. Follow the overhangs and make a delicate move into a prominent two-inch "hand and foot" jam crack extending about 100 feet up the blank face. The traverse of the NE

Farce crosses near the bottom of this crack to the deep wide crack on the right. At the top of the jam crack the two routes merge for a short distance. Then the Farce angles left on easier rock while El Whampo continues up across a smooth face protected by a bolt. The routes join at the crossing of the overhang near the summit. (1964; R. Coats, L. Reynolds, D. McLean, D. Ross)

4. EL GRANDOTE   Class 5.9   6 hours

FA: May 1961; Y. Chouinard, H. Daley

This is one of the finest routes on the north side of Tahquitz Rock. Direct aid was used at several points on early ascents. The first free ascent was made by R. Kamps and TM Herbert in 1963. The location of the route is given in the earlier descriptions of the Northeast Face and its routes. El Grandote starts directly below the conspicuous overhang. Climb up under the overhang at its left edge. Pass the overhang using the vertical wall to the left. If climbed directly below the overhang, this wall is strenuous 5.9, but if ascended about 30 feet lower it is only 5.6 in difficulty. Continue up for 150 feet where progress is blocked by another overhang which extends diagonally up and right for some distance. The cracks leading to this point are discontinuous and a free ascent requires careful route finding.

Traverse right below the overhang. It is difficult to climb free if one stays too close under the overhang. Protection is meager but adequate. Continue up and right on interesting cracks until a final undercling lieback leads around a corner to the lower end of a small but prominent gully not visible from the left. The gully leads to the upper overhang that extends from the Northeast Farce on the left to the Lark on the right. Although it is easier to join the Northeast Farce and cross the overhangs just to the left, it is considered more proper (what this really means is more difficult) to traverse right about 50 feet to a point midway between the Northeast Farce and Northeast Face. Ascent of the overhang is the last real difficulty, with class 4 pitches leading left to the Notches. Many chocks of all sizes are needed.

VARIATION 1

An interesting variation avoids the long traverse right under the middle overhang, substituting a 5.7 ascent of the overhang to the third belay ledge of the Northeast Farce. From that point traverse far right under one of two small overhangs. Protection is more easily placed along the upper overhang. This leads to the middle of the gully described in the regular route. (FA unknown)

VARIATION 2—EL DORADO

This variation starts about 150 feet to the right of the regular route. Climb 3rd class rock to a broken ledge with a medium sized sugar pine. Ascend just right of the tree, keeping right and above an arch extending down from the great overhang of El Grandote. A difficult thin crack leads up and left to a belay ledge 150 feet above. Two or three bolts and a few chocks protect this pitch. Continue up past two small interesting overhangs, keeping to the right of El Grandote as long as possible. Eventually join El Grandote near the middle overhang. (1963; T. Higgins, R. Coats)

5. NORTHEAST FACE   Class 5.6   4 hours

FA: September 1954; D. Wilson, R. Robbins

The lower half of the Northeast Face consists of smooth faces with only two prominent breaks. The right one of these is a four- to six-foot step which forms a shallow right angle wall running more than half way up the rock. The rock to the left (east) is higher than the face to the right. This shows up clearly as a discontinuous bright streak in the photograph of the north face, and can also be easily identified from the base of the North Buttress. Start a few feet to the right of the wall, where a sugar pine is found on a broad ledge 30 feet above the talus. Climb up and traverse left to the dihedral which is followed nearly to the summit. Near the top the dihedral disappears and a minor overhang is ascended directly to easier scrambling. A half dozen chocks should be sufficient.

VARIATION 1

The photograph of the North Face shows a second prominent break in the face consisting of a deep crack which extends up and right, nearly intersecting the crack of the regular route a short distance above its midpoint. The base of the crack is found near the two prominent scree gullies just right of the Northeast Rib. Near the mouth of the gully and about 200 feet right of the El Grandote overhang (Route 4) there is a large prominent sugar pine. Directly above this tree, ascend the prominent deep crack leading straight up. Follow this crack until free climbing becomes difficult. A long delicate descending traverse to the right leads to the dihedral of the main route at about the midway point. One pitch from the bottom, an alternate crack leads up and left to the upper pitches of El Dorado or El Grandote. (C. & E. Wilts)

VARIATION 2—GRACE SLICK   Class 5.10

This difficult variation ascends the rather smooth face between the two regular Northeast Face routes. Start at the top of the broken pedestal above and to the right of a large dead pine. Move left and up along a prominent crack to a medium sized mountain mahogany at the base of a large dihedral. Climb over the dihedral onto the face above and left. Beyond this point, protection is provided by five bolts as the route makes its way up the smooth face to the junction of the other two routes. For a more appropriate difficult ending, traverse left into an obvious dihedral instead of moving right to the regular Northeast Face route. (1975; J. Wilson, P. Wilkening, C. Wegener)

6. TOE BIAS   Class 5.9   5 hours

FA: June 1966; R. Kamps, B. Couch, T. Higgins

Toe Bias is an excellent exercise in difficult edging and friction which ascends the open face between the Northeast Face and the Lark. Begin 15 or 20 feet right of Route 5, ascending a rather blank face. Follow a thin crack until a traverse leads right and up (class 5.9) to a belay ledge. Above this point, climbing does not exceed 5.8, although climbing of this difficulty will be found on each of the next three pitches.

Climb over the roof above and continue up on delicate holds. A diagonal traverse reaches a lieback flake which leads to a second small belay ledge. Lieback up to and over another roof and follow a difficult crack for 100 feet to a third belay ledge. Continue up somewhat left to reach some small arches. Delicate climbing over a loose block to the right leads to easy class 4 climbing below the summit. Take plenty of chocks; if pitons are used include several knife-blades.

Variations have been reported to the right near the Lark ranging from 5.7 to 5.8 in difficulty. A specific route description is rather artificial because of the broken nature of the face near the Lark, but a climber can work out a number of interesting combinations. (G. Conner, L. de Angelo, J. Hoagland)

7. THE LARK   Class 5.3   4–5 hours

FA: November 1950; C. & E. Wilts, G. Harr, B. Tory

The Lark and its variations lie on the smooth face just left of the North Buttress. Since the regular route is not well defined by a single system of cracks, many climbers have difficulty finding the easiest route. This doesn't mean they are lost, just that they get to enjoy more difficult climbing.

On the left side of the North Buttress there is a small but prominent right angle recess or dihedral, with the right side forming the left flank of the buttress. Ascend an easy crack here for about 50 feet and traverse diagonally left and up along easy ledges for about 150 feet. Here the route proceeds directly up for several pitches. The climbing is relatively easy but the belay spots are meager. On the third or fourth pitch, the crack leading up appears more difficult and may be bypassed by a short traverse left to an easier right angle dihedral. Near the top the route passes a lone sprawling lodgepole pine (two needles to the bundle)—the only one on the rock known to the editor—and then tends slightly right finally entering the left side of a prominent chute which is readily seen from the bottom. Either the left side or the dead end of the chute may be ascended to the top. An average collection of four or five chocks is adequate.

VARIATION 1—WEST LARK   Class 5.5

There are two crack systems in the recess or dihedral at the start of the Lark. The right system forms the right angle of the recess, and the other is on the face ten or 20 feet left. This variation follows the latter crack system until the two merge near the summit. The climbing is often only class 4 in difficulty but several more difficult cruxes in the form of small overhangs must be overcome. The third of these is the most interesting–about class 5.5. Above this point climb out of a narrow chute to make a delicate exposed traverse left to join the regular route just below the deep chute at the top. (1954; R. Gorin, J. Hudson, W. Dixon, E. Wilts)

An obscure variation bears left just below the last crux. If it is found, it gives a route even easier than the regular (East) Lark route.

VARIATION 2—HARD LARK   Class 5.7

The Hard Lark is a variation that ascends the face just left of the West Lark. For a more interesting beginning, climb the face to the left and cross the Lark on the diagonal traverse. The next pitch ascends the smooth face to a short lieback and thin arch which is climbed directly. Continue up, paralleling the West Lark until the summit chute is reached. (1966; B. Berry, J. Williams)

8. THE UNEVENTFUL   Class 5.5   4 hours

FA: October 1959; H. Daley, Y. Chouinard, C. Butler, D. Doody

The North Buttress is a split buttress at the bottom, having two distinct ridges with a shallow gully between. The Uneventful follows the left ridge, staying on the crest and passing two solitary pine trees. The two ridges of the buttress merge in a broken area marked by two large pine trees, one of which has an unusual shape. At this point, Route 9 on the North Buttress is crossed. Climbing below this point is not more than 5.4 in difficulty. Directly above the upper tree is an interesting 5.5 chimney which leads to easier pitches and the top of the rock. Alternatively, Route 9 may be followed for a class 5.3 finish. About ten chocks for the entire climb.

VARIATION 1—HUBRIS   Class 5.10

Anything but uneventful, this is a challenging 5.10 face climb on the narrow left flank of the North Buttress. Start 30 feet right of the West Lark and ascend an obvious left leaning lieback flake 40 feet until just above a small roof. Traverse left on a narrow ledge and up to a bolt near the left edge of the face. Continue up past another bolt and a small bush to a belay with two bolts. Continue up the left edge of the flake with lieback, face climbing and narrow cracks until level with the first large pine tree on the North Buttress. Traverse right to join the Uneventful. A few wired chocks should be carried. (1974; M. Gonzalez, M. Heath)

THE NORTH FACE

ROUTES 9–18

The North Face of Tahquitz Rock is a few hundred yards wide and extends from the North Buttress on the left to the Northwest Buttress on the right. The North Buttress is rather poorly defined, consisting of a shallow projection on the north side of the rock. In the photograph of the North Face, the North Buttress is near the center of the picture, bounded on the left by a wide shadow extending to the top of the rock. The buttress can be readily identified since the base of the rock dips sharply on approaching from the right, and then extends nearly horizontally to the scree chutes near the Northeast Rib.

The Northwest Buttress is much more prominent. It forms the left skyline of the rock when viewed from Lunch Rock. In the photograph of the North Face, the Northwest Buttress is near the right side of the picture, bordered on the left by a deep shadow which extends halfway up the rock. Between the two buttresses lie nine or ten of the longer routes on the rock. Just right of the North Buttress is a shallow recess or chute. The Error (Route 10) is at the left-hand edge of the chute and the Sahara Terror (Route 11) is 30 or 40 feet to the right near the right hand edge. Farther right, the North Face is hollowed deeply just left of the Northwest Buttress. This forms a much wider recess about 200 feet wide called the Northwest Recess. Four prominent vertical cracks are found in this recess, comprising four of the next five routes—from left to right the Hoodenett, Swallow, Consolation and Long Climb (Routes 13 to 17). The cracks lie so close that interconnection at several points is possible, but each route is quite distinct and offers a different class of climbing problems. Up on the left flank of the Northwest Buttress and just right of the Long Climb is the Illegitimate (Route 18).

9. NORTH BUTTRESS   Class 5.3   3 hours

FA: August 1952; R. Smith, D. Wilson

The North Buttress is a split buttress at the bottom, having two distinct ridges. This route stays on the right side of the right ridge until they merge. Several pitches on easy low angle slabs lead to this point which is marked by two large pine trees high on the buttress. The upper tree has a very unusual shape so that this point can be readily identified. This marks the beginning of more difficult climbing; from here, many climbers miss the easiest route. From the lower of the two trees, traverse about 40 feet left and up along a broken ledge. Cross a 30-foot smooth face left on small holds. Evidently most climbers miss this crossing, expecting the footholds to be larger or more obvious. It is at the same level as the upper of the two trees. Those who miss the crossing and continue up encounter distressingly difficult climbing above.

From the end of the traverse, ascend straight up a shallow gully and then over broken rock to the East Ridge. This route was rated 5.0 in earlier editions. I agree with this rating up to the two large pine trees but the upper section involves moves of at least 5.3 in difficulty. One or two chocks if no problems in route finding.

10. THE ERROR   Class 5.6   4 hours

FA: September 1952; G. Hemming, J. Gallwas, B. Lilley, G. Schlief

The shallow chute just right of the North Buttress is blocked by a large overhang about 200 feet from the bottom. Above this point the chute branches with the left branch leading diagonally left to the two trees high on the North Buttress (Route 9). Easy climbing up the left edge of the chute leads to the overhang which is passed most easily by traversing right about 30 feet. Traverse back left and follow the left branch of the chute to the North Buttress Route which can be followed to the top. Three or four chocks are suggested.

11. SAHARA TERROR   Class 5.6   5 hours

FA: July 1942; W. Shand, R. Gorin, P. Flinchbaugh

The name of this route is considered a misnomer by most climbers since the north side of the rock generally provides the coolest climbing. However, the first ascent partly attached this name because of the extreme heat and dryness experienced there on a very hot day in July. Originally climbed with aid, the first free ascent was made by W. Pabst and S. Austin.

The route starts just right of the North Buttress in the same shallow chute as the Error. At the right side of the chute there is a prominent crack forming the right bottom edge of the chute, and about ten to 15 feet left is another crack. The Sahara Terror follows the latter crack for two or three pitches. This crack may be ascended from the bottom, or if approaching from the right, it is a little shorter to traverse across a rock apron to reach the crack about 100 feet above the base.

Ascend the crack over a slight overhang to a prominent small mountain mahogany. Continue up 15 or 20 feet and traverse right along a deep dog-leg crack. Again climb straight up for two pitches until progress is blocked by slight overhangs. Traverse back left about ten feet around a corner and ascend the slight overhang. Continue up diagonally left 50 feet in a shallow crack or gully. Now climb up and right across a difficult broken face to the base of a 40-foot shallow wide chimney. This leads into a deeper gully with easy pitches leading to the east summit ridge a short distance above the Notches.

This route is a little more detailed than the editor would prefer, but a number of climbers have complained about difficulty in route finding on the upper pitches. If one or two fixed pins are in place, about eight chocks will be needed.

12. MAGICAL MYSTERY TOUR   Class 5.11

FA: D. Evans, M. Graham, M. Cox, T. Sorenson, J. Wilson

With a name like this it is inappropriate to say more than that the route ascends the difficult buttress between the Sahara Terror and Hoodenett. Originally reported as a 5.10 A3 aid climb, the first free ascent was made by M. Cox in July 1976.

13. THE HOODENETT   Class 5.9   5 hours

FA: September 1957; J. Fitschen, R. Robbins

The name of this route is derived from the fact that the first ascent party found an old piton in place halfway up the rock, and in view of the difficulty asked, "Who done it?" The rock follows for most of its length a prominent crack or dihedral formed by the juncture of the face of the Northwest Recess and the bordering buttress on the left. It is right of the Sahara Terror (Route 11) and just to the left of the Swallow. The main crack begins 150 feet above the base of the rock. To reach this crack, start in the middle of the apron between the left edge of the recess and the small central buttress. Ascend diagonally left and up for about 120 feet to a point below the main crack. An easy vertical A1 crack is usually ascended at this point, but T. Higgins and R. Kamps in 1966 found that the pitch could be climbed free requiring one 5.9 move. Above this point the climbing does not exceed 5.8 in difficulty. The route enters the main dihedral and stays generally in this crack until the crack ends just beneath some overhangs near the summit of the rock. The overhangs are ascended through a weakness just to the right with one more class 5 pitch leading directly to the summit. A large number of thin to medium chocks will be used.

Two or three pitches below the summit, the route passes the trunk of a large dead mountain mahogany. Just below this spot is the left end of the ledge system described in the next route which crosses the entire Northwest Recess.

14. THE SWALLOW   Class 5.8   5 hours

FA: June 1952; C. Wilts, R. Robbins

The Swallow for most of its length follows the first continuous vertical crack system to the right of the Hoodenett. It starts just left of a small 150-foot buttress in the center of the Northwest Recess. Easy climbing on the right side of a steep apron leads to a headwall about 200 feet above the base of the rock. At this point the Swallow makes a loop to the left, just touching the Hoodenett, then diagonally up and back to the right, returning to the original crack system. Ascend directly for two or three pitches (including a strenuous jam crack and a short 5.7 overhang) to a ledge on the left which slopes downward to the Hoodenett. A small twisted shrub tree will be found on this ledge. Just above the ledge, ascend on the right side of a 20-foot tall triangular block of rock. From the top of this block, climb a strenuous vertical crack and then continue on less steep rock to a broad ledge. This ledge extends from the left at a point just below the dead tree on the Hoodenett across the Swallow and Consolation, continuing right just above a large mountain mahogany around a small point to a small white fir on the Long Climb, and then leads over to the last two pitches of the White Maiden. This is the main ledge across the upper part of the Northwest Recess and can be used to connect the upper and lower pitches of the seven routes found here. The best ending for the Swallow is to continue up past one more small mountain mahogany, diagonal right, and then climb up under the summit overhangs. Cut back left and ascend the overhangs with the Hoodenett.

VARIATION 1—THE GULP   Class 5.9

Following the tradition established with other routes (e.g., the Long Climb and the Jam Crack), this is an attempt to establish a route that zigzags across the Swallow but uses as little of this route as possible. Although the Swallow was named because of the unusual abundance of swallows flying nearby on the occasion of the first ascent, the climbers of the variation chose to misinterpret the name so that they could call the variation the Gulp.

Climb the first two pitches of the Swallow and continue in the crack system up the small headwall instead of making the loop to the left. Where the Swallow returns along a sloping ledge on the left, descend left along this ledge five or ten feet and then ascend the face at a small crack. Continue up a jam crack midway between the Swallow and Hoodenett, following around to the left of a small vertical wall. Above this point continue in the crack for 30 feet. Here traverse right (using an underclinging lieback) to the Swallow, meeting this route just below its 5.7 overhang. Ascend this overhang and follow the regular route a short distance to the ledge with the 20-foot triangular block. At this point traverse right ten feet then continue up to reach the ledge system described in the regular route. Continue up or traverse on this ledge to any of the nearby routes. (1965; P. Gerhard, D. Ross)

15. THE CONSOLATION   Class 5.9   5 hours

FA: May 1953; J. Mendenhall, C. Wilts

The Consolation lies in the central cracks of the Northwest Recess, starting on the right side of a small 150-foot buttress. Jam cracks and liebacks lead directly up for several pitches which become progressively more difficult. Between the two most difficult pitches, a ledge broadens to the right and leads to the Long Climb (Route 17). Above the second of these pitches is an area where the face is less steep, the rock more broken and a number of rather large mountain mahogany are found. A short pitch here leads to the ledge system described in Route 14 which cuts across the entire Northwest Recess. One can traverse either way to adjacent routes, but the recommended route is to continue straight up just right of a small mountain mahogany, and then ascend diagonally right to a weak spot in the summit overhangs.

   On the first ascent, excessive water on the rock forced the use of aid. The first complete free ascent was made by R. Robbins and TM Herbert. About a dozen chocks.

16. THE SHAM   Class 5.10 & A2   6 hours

FA: May 1964; T. Higgins, R. Coats

The Sham is a somewhat artificial climb in which the climber is restricted to the smooth face between the Consolation and the Long Climb. On the first ascent, Higgins and Coats traversed right from the first bolt to the Wong Climb to finish the first pitch. They were also unable to finish the third pitch due to excessive water on the rock. The first as-

cent of the complete route was made by R. Kamps and
B. Powell. Ascend more or less on the first pitch of the Consolation to a sturdy bush just below the first level of overhangs. Above this point lieback up and right onto a spectacular face. Pass right of a slight overhang and ascend a flake
up to and over its end (5.10), or considerably easier bypass
the flake on the right. Above this point an expansion anchor protects a very difficult (5.10+) traverse left and up to
a belay ledge.

The second pitch starts 15 or 20 feet left of the Mummy
Crack of the Long Climb and ascends an obvious direct aid
crack system (one expansion anchor) to a vertical chimney
which leads to a second belay ledge. The third pitch continues straight up a vertical crack followed by a dihedral, with
fairly continuous 5.8 climbing near the top. From the broad
ledge at the top of this pitch, complete the ascent by joining
the Consolation or the Long Climb. This route may require
a few pitons in addition to a good chock assortment.

17. THE LONG CLIMB   Class 5.7   5 hours

FA: May 1952; R. Robbins, D. Wilson

From the right-hand corner of the Northwest Recess, ascend the rock apron to the conspicuous wide crack or chimney at the extreme right. Ascend one pitch and traverse left
out of the top of this crack to a broad ledge. Twenty feet left
of the starting crack is the "Mummy Crack," a 50-foot chimney barely large enough to enter. Above the chimney lies
broken rock on the right and above this is a slight overhang,
leading to another and broader ledge. This is the ledge
found on the Consolation, which serves as the belay posi-

tion between its two most difficult pitches. The next pitch starts at the right end of this ledge, ascending rather poor rock to a second overhang and ending at an unusually large specimen of mountain mahogany. Another short pitch leads up and slightly right to a small ten-foot white fir which cannot be seen from below. This point is on the main ledge system described in Route 14, The Swallow, which cuts across the entire Northwest Recess. From here it is possible to traverse either way to other routes. An interesting ending continues straight up the gully above the fir. Pass on the left side of an overhanging downward-jutting block speckled with black lichen. Above this go right ten feet then straight up an ill-defined crack to a V-notch. Easy climbing leads to the summit.

VARIATION 1—THE WONG CLIMB   Class 5.8

The Wong Climb is a more difficult variation of the first two pitches of the Long Climb. Ascend the first crack to the left of the first pitch of the Long Climb. At the first belay ledge where the Long Climb traverses left to the Mummy Crack, this route traverses right and ascends the awkward chimney avoided by the traverse of the regular route. Some care is required on the second pitch because of a few loose chockstones. Continue to the summit as in Route 17. (1963; T. Higgins, D. Molner, R. Coats)

18. THE ILLEGITIMATE   Class 5.9   6 hours

FA: May 1959; TM Herbert, R. Robbins

The Illegitimate derives its name from the extremely improbable appearance of the route. It starts on the left side of the Northwest Buttress about 20 feet to the right of a young sugar pine growing just below the start of the Long Climb. Move right and up through a broken area and shrub trees to a long crack which leads 200 feet diagonally up and left on the left side of the buttress. Because of the length of this crack, it is necessary to belay from slings part way up. A small overhang awaits the climber at the end of this crack and is followed by the crux pitch on which the climbing is both delicate and strenuous. Climb directly up using small holds and cracks to a point 15 feet below a sharp overhang where the route diagonals around to the right following a difficult crack and a delicate traverse to a belay. From here a lieback leads directly up to a sturdy tree. Above easy class 4 climbing leads to the main ledge system across the North-west Recess. The route may be finished by using the upper pitches of any of the adjacent climbs.

THE NORTHWEST FACE

ROUTES 19–53

More than 35 routes are found on the broad Northwest Face which extends from the Northwest Buttress to the West Buttress. This is the portion of the rock that can be seen from Lunch Rock. The left skyline is the Northwest Buttress. The White Maiden's Walkaway (Route 19) ascends this buttress. Running diagonally up and to the right and nearly bisecting the face is the deep gully called the Trough (Route 32). Between this and the Northwest Buttress the upper part of the rock forms a large rounded bulge which is cut just left of center by a deep crack which forms the Super Pooper (Route 23). Between the White Maiden and this route lie from left to right the Fool's Rush gully, the dihedral of the Step and the overhanging roof of Le Toit. To the right of the Super Pooper on the open face of the bulge lie three of the finest West Face routes, the Flakes, Stairway to Heaven and the Vampire. To the right of the Trough about 200 feet, a lesser gully or cleft cuts the face. This is the Angel's Fright (Route 39) which runs more or less parallel to the Trough. Seven or eight routes are found between these. Just right of the Angel's Fright, the rock has broken away to form an overhanging arch which is vertical at the bottom, but arches over to the right to meet a similar arch from the far right. The underside of these arches form the Human Fright (Route 41) and the Finger-trip (Route 45) respectively. The Switchbacks and Blanket-ty-Blank wander about on the steep face between. Just above and right of the right arch is the sloping ledge which forms the Fingertip Traverse (Route 46). Between this and the West Buttress are several closely spaced routes, and the buttress itself is ascended by several routes including the Traitor Horn and the Last Judgment.

19. WHITE MAIDEN'S WALKAWAY

Class 5.1   **3 hours**

FA: August 1937; J. Smith, A. Johnson

The White Maiden's Walkaway, more often simply called the White Maiden, is one of the most popular routes for inexperienced groups. Its relative ease and greater than average length make it ideal for a beginner's introduction to serious climbing. Since it is frequently ascended by relative beginners and since the route is long and somewhat obscure the description is more detailed than might seem necessary to the advanced climber.

   The route lies generally on the Northwest Buttress which forms the left skyline of Tahquitz Rock when viewed from Lunch Rock. One-third of the way up the buttress is a conspicuous rock tooth or gendarme. Climb to this tooth by one of several routes. The easiest lies on the far left side of the buttress. Ascend scree on the left side of the buttress into the base of the Northwest Recess (see North Face Routes).

The last tree here is a lone medium-sized sugar pine. From a point near this tree, climb diagonally right into an easy crack or chute (or else ascend the crack from its bottom). Climb past a medium-sized sugar pine and up to a dense shrubby area next to a rock tooth on the right. Beyond these shrubs traverse right (west) across a face six feet to enter the "Walkaway," a prominent deep crack at the base of a six-foot wall on the right. Follow this crack up along the left side of the buttress, reaching the skyline at the gendarme.

A more interesting approach is up a shallow chute starting at the lowest point of the buttress. This leads through a vertical tunnel after which one continues up the bottom of the chute another 50 feet to the shrubby area described in the first route. A third more difficult variation leads directly to the tooth by way of a deep chimney on the right side of the buttress.

Above this point the Northwest Buttress widens into a broad face. Most errors in route finding are made in the next two or three pitches. Ascend 20 feet to a good belay stance on the crest of the buttress. (Incidentally this is the starting or finishing point for From Bad Traverse.) A shallow open gully leads up on the left. Ascend this gully using some good hidden handholds to a ledge with several bushes and a small tree. A smaller gully farther left may also be used on this pitch, but the climbing is more difficult. Move to the left end of the ledge and continue up one more short pitch. Where easy climbing is blocked, traverse left a few feet around "Doubtful Corner" and climb up past a large mountain mahogany. Continue straight up on 4th class pitches for about 150 feet and then walk up an easy crack or gully that leads diagonally up and right. Where this gully ends, the remaining pitch can be ascended in three ways. The easiest (5.0) requires a traverse past a very small tree and along a fingertip ledge far out to the right and then an ascent of easy friction to the end of the climb. The most difficult (5.7) is straight up the overhang above. The third is about class 5.3 in difficulty and lies between the other two. Most parties complete this route using two to four chocks.

An interesting variation of this route, called the "White Maiden Direct" stays on the center of the buttress instead of traversing left at the first ledge above the gendarme. This variation requires one or two additional chocks and is about class 5.3 in difficulty.

20. FOOL'S RUSH   Class 5.6   5 hours

FA: O. Conger, B. Lilley, D. Rappolee

Just right of the Northwest Buttress lies a prominent chute or dihedral which extends far up the rock. The chute is shallow near the lower end where it crosses From Bad Traverse (Route 28) and below it merges into a wide trough near the base of the rock. This trough separates the Northwest Buttress on the left and the 150-foot buttress described in Routes 21 or 22. Ascend the left side of this trough and enter the dihedral at the crossing of From Bad Traverse. Climbing becomes progressively more difficult until an overhang is reached which is most easily passed on the right. Above this point it is possible to make an easy traverse to the White Maiden. It is, however, more interesting to stay on the Fool's Rush by jogging right a few feet and continuing straight up. The White Maiden is finally joined at the last pitch.

21. THE STEP   Class 5.9   5 hours

FA: July 1957; J. Gallwas, R. Robbins

The Step follows the small but prominent crack that divides the face between the Northwest Buttress and the great bulge of the West Face. Originally climbed with aid, the first free ascent was made by TM Herbert and R. Robbins. A prominent buttress at the base of the West Face is located midway between the White Maiden and the Trough. This buttress is about 150 feet high and is topped by a broad ledge and a large pine tree. The route starts in the trough between this buttress on the right and the Northwest Buttress on the left, staying close to the former. At the top of the buttress, cross From Bad Traverse about 50 feet right of the Fool's Rush. Here the route enters a small but prominent dihedral topped by a sharp overhang (particularly on the right). Part way up this dihedral is a small tree where an awkward belay can be established. This procedure is recommended to ensure enough rope for the leader to reach the next good belay stance.

The next pitch is the most difficult on the route, offering few opportunities for the climber to rest. Above this pitch the route is straightforward, tending to the right to avoid the Fool's Rush. An overhang which arches slightly to the right is passed by moving diagonally right and then back on 5.8 holds and cracks. Near the top of this pitch, the "Step," a foot long platform, is encountered. Easier climbing leads to the West Shoulder.

This route has been rated 5.8 for 20 years. I have heard

indirectly that recent changes on the rock have raised the difficulty at least to 5.9, but I have no direct verification. In any case, take plenty of chocks.

22. LE TOIT   Class 5.11   5 hours

FA: March 1960; TM Herbert, T. Frost, Y. Chouinard

Le Toit derives its name from the large overhang or "roof" which can be seen high up on the West Face near the Northwest Buttress. The principal challenge of the route is to surmount this roof at its widest point. It was originally ascended with aid below and above the roof as well as on the crossing of the roof. For more than ten years it ranked with the Green Arch as one of the favorite aid routes (class A3). The first free ascent was made in 1973 by J. Long and R. Accomazzo. Most climbers will still want to use aid—at least on the roof itself.

The simplest approach is to cross either way along From Bad Traverse, but the approach described below is much more appropriate considering the difficulty of the route above. A prominent buttress at the base of the West Face has been described in the previous route. Ascend this buttress directly. The first 100 feet are easy, but they lead to an unlikely looking lieback up a left facing dihedral on the left side of the buttress (class 5.8). This leads to the top of the buttress where From Bad Traverse is crossed.

Climb the headwall above, staying well to the right of the deep angle or dihedral in which the Step is found. Some 5.9 moves and finally a 5.10 undercling brings one to the crux of the climb, Le Toit itself. The 5.11 climbing over the overhang is not only strenuous, but difficult to protect. Above interesting face climbing leads to a small belay bush.

Continue on difficult 5.10 face climbing up and to the right under a small arch until it is possible to climb over the arch. Continue directly up on spectacular but easy free climbing to a ledge from which one can traverse into the Step on the left or the Super Pooper on the right. Take plenty of nuts, including several small stoppers.

23. SUPER POOPER   Class 5.9   5 hours

FA: September 1952; C. Wilts, D. Wilson,
    J. & R. Mendenhall

Between the Northwest Buttress and the Trough, the upper part of Tahquitz Rock forms a large bulge which is cut left of center by a prominent deep cleft. The Super Pooper follows this cleft. The simplest approach is to ascend From Bad Traverse to the top of the prominent 150-foot buttress midway between the Trough and the White Maiden. Those desiring a longer route of comparable difficulty will find an interesting direct approach on the face of this buttress. About 20 feet right of the dihedral described in Le Toit is a prominent crack leading directly up. It is described as a spooky class 5.7 lead but the protection is good. Continue across the From Bad Traverse to the deep cleft in the upper bulge of the West Face.

The entrance to the cleft is the most difficult pitch on the route. For 15 years direct aid was used at this point, but R. Kamps and M. Powell achieved the first free ascent in 1967. Ascend the steep V-trough on the right then move out on the face and up six feet to a very small ledge. A difficult right hand jam permits the move off the ledge. Continue up the jam crack and exit to the left to relatively easy climbing. The upper part of the route is quite obvious.

Climbing becomes progressively more difficult, the last two pitches being particularly interesting. On the last pitch, climbing is blocked by a vertical wall. A delicate traverse around the corner on the right leads to a weakness where the wall may be ascended directly. Take a good selection of chocks.

A challenging direct aid variation to the last two pitches has been found by M. Prodanovitch and S. McKinney. Pitons are recommended here until the aid crack will accept stoppers. The next-to-last pitch of the regular route is a lieback which extends up to a small overhang usually passed on the left to further lieback climbing. The variation starts at the overhang. Move up and right, traversing on good holds directly across the face of a green headwall. This traverse ends at the edge of the huge arch which is directly above the Flakes and the Vampire. The exposure at this point is particularly exhilarating. Directly above is a crack which parallels the arch about eight inches from its lip. Nail up the crack which gets progressively poorer until it disappears. From the last aid pin there are no further piton cracks for the remaining 50 feet of difficult climbing.

24. THE FLAKES   Class 5.11   6 hours

FA: July 1953; R. Robbins, D. Wilson

The Flakes was another favorite aid climb for 20 years until a free ascent was pushed through in 1973 by J. Long, T. Sorenson, R. Harrison and W. Antel. The route can be approached by ascending From Bad Traverse to the top of the prominent 150-foot buttress midway between the Trough and the White Maiden (see Route 21). However those desiring a longer route of comparable difficulty will find an interesting direct approach on the right side of the buttress. At the right margin of the buttress a prominent right angle dihedral with a series of four overhangs can be seen on the photograph of the West Face. Climb directly up the dihedral, passing over all overhangs except the third which is passed by jamming up a remarkable 15-foot tunnel behind it. Continue up across From Bad Traverse to the point where the Super Pooper enters the cleft in the upper bulge of Tahquitz Rock.

Just right of the first pitch of the Super Pooper, climb straight up an easy direct aid crack ending in an overhang. This involves 5.10 climbing if done free. Above is a bushy belay at the base of a large detached flake. The face of the flake to the left is ascended to a ledge which extends farther left to the Super Pooper. Face climbing over the small bulge above is not only difficult (5.10+ or 5.11), but hard to protect without a piton. Above, continue slightly left to a short strenuous lieback leading to the base of the great arch which extends up and right above the great bulge. Diagonal up and right across the face below the arch for 80 feet and then ascend a short overhanging chimney to the last difficulty of the route, a 5.8 move up a 15-foot wall.

Although several fixed pins are in place, the piton at the crux move and another near the top cannot be driven solidly enough to remain as fixed pins. It is best to carry a couple of pitons along with a wide assortment of chocks.

VARIATION—STAIRWAY TO HEAVEN
Class 5.9 & A4

This challenging variation was worked out in September 1973 by D. Black, D. Hanbury, and M. Graber. Climb by any route to the beginning of the regular route above From Bad Traverse. Start left near the Super Pooper and ascend a four-inch lieback until aid pins are needed to reach a bolt. This protects the difficult mantle to the belay bushes on the Flakes. Instead of diagonalling left across the face of the large flake, ascend the dihedral at the right edge of the flake (5.9) to another excellent belay ledge. A hook and two aid bolts give access to difficult aid climbing up an expanding arch. At the top, traverse right to a narrow ledge and climb directly up past two aid bolts to easier climbing leading to the headwall of the arches above.

25. THE VAMPIRE   Class 5.10+   8 hours

FA: June 1959; R. Robbins, D. Rearick

This impressive spectacular climb follows a line which diagonals steeply up and left across the large smooth bulge which dominates the West Face. It is one of the most challenging routes on the rock. The first free ascent was accomplished in 1973 by J. Long, M. Graham, R. Accomazzo and W. Antel.

Climb to the base of the bulge above From Bad Traverse and right of the Super Pooper and the Flakes. From a ledge on the left margin, descend an easy crack to the right for 20 feet to reach the Bat Crack (so named because of the many bats flushed out on the first ascent of the Bat variation). An alternative approach is to climb up and left from the small fir tree on the Passover (Route 27). The Bat Crack is a difficult wide vertical open-book type crack which steadily narrows. Jam and lieback (5.10) to a point where it is possible to traverse right to a small bush and belay bolt. Climb back left and make a difficult mantle, then traverse left past a bolt to the prominent flake on the blank face. Spectacular liebacks lead under and up the left side of the flake system until the "batwalk" leads left to some belay bolts. Climb back to the flakes and continue up for two pitches to the headwall above, where the route joins the Flakes.

The ascent can be protected entirely with chocks (and fixed pins), but a remarkably wide assortment is required.

VARIATION—THE BAT   Class 5.10+

A much less strenuous variation is called the Bat. It was in fact the original route of first ascent by D. Wilson, J. Gallwas and C. Wilts. Instead of traversing left above the Bat Crack, continue up and right to a ledge and bush. Just left of this belay point follow a difficult crack to its end. Above and to its right are a couple of expansion bolts which can be used to pendulum to the right to easy climbing between the two Royal's Arches. The first free ascent (that is, free up to the last bolts) was made by T. Sorenson.

26. CHIN STRAP CRACK   Class 5.10   3 hours

FA: June 1966; C. Raymond, L. Harrell

Start the ascent as in the Passover past the small fir to the broken ledge. From its left end work up into the prominent dihedral that leads to the left end of Lower Royal's Arch. Chocks and one or two expansion bolts can be used to protect the difficult lead up the dihedral.

27. THE PASSOVER   Class 5.10   4 hours

FA: June 1964; R. Kamps, R. Coats, T. Higgins

The Passover ascends the face just left of the Trough, cross-

71

ing Lower Royal's Arch at midpoint. The "Passover" is the direct surmounting of the roof of the arch. From the beginning of From Bad Traverse in the Trough, climb up past a small fir tree to a broken ledge. From its left end climb up and right across the face. Interesting climbing leads to an expansion bolt a short distance below Lower Royal's Arch and near its left end. Difficult face climbing past the bolt is followed by a short easy lieback and a very strenuous move over the overhang of the arch. From the end of a short trough, climb left to Upper Royal's Arch or right to the last pitch of the Piton Pooper.

For ten years this route was climbed with aid (A1) at the bolt and over the Passover. The first free ascent was made by T. Sorenson and R. Accomazzo in 1973.

VARIATION—ZIGGY STARDUST   Class 5.10+

This variation is more accurately an exciting ending of the Passover. It was first ascended in 1975 by P. Wilkening and J. Wilson. In the photograph of the West Face, a thin arch can be seen extending up and right from near the left end of Lower Royal's Arch. Midway through the overhang of the Passover, climb around the block to the right to enter this arch. Near the end of the arch a hanging belay can be established using fixed pins and small stoppers. Follow the crack to the right and above until it joins the Piton Pooper at the top of its first pitch. Both pitches of this variation are 5.10 in difficulty.

28. FROM BAD TRAVERSE   Class 4   1 hour

FA: September 1939; R. Brinton, H. Fuller

This route, whose name is an almost unspeakable pun by Bob Brinton, offers an easy 4th class traverse from the top of the first pitch on the Trough (Route 32) to the top of the second or third pitch of the White Maiden (Route 19). It is crossed by or can serve as the starting point for several routes on the face between these two.

From the platform at the top of the first pitch of the Trough traverse left and upward for two or three pitches, passing bushes and several trees on the way. This reaches the large ledge on top of the 150-foot buttress midway between the Trough and White Maiden. This ledge is covered with buckthorn and has as its principal landmark a large pine tree. From here the route dips slightly as it continues left and then climbs slightly to the notch behind the gendarme on the White Maiden which shows up so prominently when viewed from Lunch Rock.

29. ROYAL'S ARCHES

These routes were named in 1952 before either arch had been climbed, with the hope that Robbins would participate in the first ascent of each arch. The lower arch consists of the sharp overhangs to the left of Pine Tree Ledge of the Trough. The upper arch lies 100 or 200 feet above, forming the right boundary of the great bulge on the West Face.

a. LOWER ARCH   Class 5.10+

FA: May 1952; R. Robbins, D. Wilson, C. Wilts

This route was considered an excellent exercise in piton placement (A2) for 20 years, until T. Sorenson and R. Accomazzo climbed it free in 1973. Starting in the Trough, just below the left end of Pine Tree Ledge, traverse left under the overhangs. The difficult lieback or undercling moves can be adequately protected by nuts if one or two fixed pins are in place. At the end of the overhangs climb directly up to a good belay ledge. The next pitch leads straight up to a small well-formed sugar pine which marks the lower end of the Upper Arch.

b. UPPER ARCH   Class 5.7

FA: 1953; R. Robbins, J. Gallwas, C. Wilts

The Upper Arch begins at the small sugar pine that marks the end of the previous route. This point may also be reached by 3rd class cracks and ledges leading down and left from the West Shoulder. The arch has been formed by the breaking away of exfoliation slabs on the steep face, forming an overhanging arch very similar to the Fingertrip. The route ascends under the arch, occasionally on the face. Ascend the overhang at the top where the route joins the Flakes.

30. PITON POOPER   Class 5.7   2 hours

FA: September 1936; R. Brinton, A. Johnson

In the early years at Tahquitz, this route was considered the classic direct aid route, requiring many pitons for a piton ladder on the first pitch—hence the name. The first free ascent was made in 1949 by C. and E. Wilts and S. Austin. In view of its current rating, the name is no longer appropriate. Leave the Trough at Pine Tree Ledge. Traverse a few feet to the left on a narrow ledge into a prominent crack. Ascend up the crack and the face to its left for 30 feet to a small scrubby pine growing in a crack on the vertical face. From this point stay close to the right wall along an arch, lying back on the crack there all the way over a slight overhang. Above this continue straight up toward the large overhanging arch at the top of the route, which can be turned either to the left or the right on smooth friction pitches.

31. GALLWAS' GALLOP   Class 5.9   2 hours

FA: 1953; J. Gallwas, C. Wilts, R. Robbins

The Gallwas Gallop starts at the Pine Tree Ledge of the Trough. Just left of the sugar pine, ascend the steep face where it is broken by one or two cracks leading upward. Two interesting (i.e., difficult) spots will be encountered about 40 feet and 60 feet above the ledge. The first pitch is ended by climbing diagonally right to a ledge large enough for a belay. Above, an interesting jam crack leads to easy scrambling to the West Shoulder.

32. THE TROUGH   Class 5.0   2 hours

FA: August 1936; J. Smith, R. Brinton, Z. Jasaitis

The Trough is the easiest route that ascends the face of Tahquitz Rock. It is an important route historically since it is the first one found on the Rock, but is even more important as a training route since it is an ideal introduction to climbing for the dubious beginner.

The Trough is the prominent gully bearing slightly

75

right from the vertical which divides the Northwest Face into roughly equal parts. It is best approached by ascending directly to the rock from Lunch Rock and traversing left along the base for about 100 yards. It is possible to make a direct ascent of the main gully below this point, but it is much more difficult. The first pitch ascends 60 or 70 feet up a narrow crack on the right side of the trough to a platform with a large block above. Climb left around the block and ascend a chimney on its left side. A short distance above this point the exposure and climbing difficulty increase so that a chock may be advisable. Above this point the trough deepens and 100 feet of easy climbing ends at a slight overhang. Climb out to the right on smooth slabs onto a large ledge with a prominent sugar pine. This prominent ledge is frequently used as a reference point in other route descriptions. The Rack, Jam Crack and Frightful Variation terminate and the Piton Pooper, Royal's Arches, Gallwas' Gallop and Swing Traverse start at this ledge. From the large tree continue diagonally upward and right. The trough continues to the West Shoulder with mixed 3rd and 4th class pitches. Two chocks.

VARIATION—THE RACK   Class 5.9

A very interesting variation was found in 1961 by R. Kamps, M. and B. Powell. It is particularly recommended for those who want a more interesting approach to the Piton Pooper or Gallwas Gallop. The Rack lies on the narrow face to the right of the Trough. The route is at all times just a few feet from the gully forming the Trough. At the bottom of the crack which is the usual first pitch of the Trough, climb up on the face to the right and continue climbing a small crack to a bush about 80 feet up. Two expansion anchors are in place for protection on this pitch. Above the bush a short lieback leads to the right around an overhang to a small steep trough which is followed to another small overhang. Above this continue up another trough to a belay ledge on the left. The last pitch goes in a direct line to the tree on Pine Tree Ledge of the Trough where this route ends.

33. THE JAM CRACK   Class 5.7   3 hours

FA: September 1959; D. Wilson, R. Robbins

The Jam Crack route begins immediately to the right of the Trough. About 30 feet from the ground, cross left around a corner and over an overhang to enter the jam crack. This crack ends in a larger overhang which is regarded by most as the crux of the climb although the jam crack below is actually more strenuous. Easier climbing finishes the pitch at a ledge a full 100 feet from the start.

   Traverse right to a short lieback and then continue up on delicate face climbing with some lack of protection. Here a traverse right can be used to join the Frightful Variation (Route 37), but a more interesting continuation traverses left under an overhang on delicate friction to a ledge near the Trough. Climb up and right to reach Pine Tree Ledge on the Trough.

VARIATION—DAVE'S DEVIATION   Class 5.10

A more difficult variation starts and ends at the same points, but zigzags oppositely. At the start of the Jam Crack, climb diagonally up the face to the right to the second of two very small trees. Above is a difficult two-inch vertical crack which is climbed directly to a belay ledge. The Jam Crack route crosses this ledge from the left and goes straight up. Dave's Deviation does the opposite, crossing the ledge to the left and continuing up a right angle gully at that end. From a ledge at the end of this gully diagonal right beneath a small overhanging arch and up to a poor belay spot beneath another overhang. At this point there is once again an intersection with the Jam Crack, the latter route traversing left. Either join the Jam Crack or continue on more difficult rock to the right to reach Pine Tree Ledge. The first complete ascent of the variation was made by T. Frost and R. Robbins in 1960.

34. DEVIL'S DELIGHT   Class 5.9   5 hours

FA: August 1966; M. and B. Powell

Although somewhat artificial because of its nearness to the Frightful Variation, this is an excellent route for sustained climbing in the 5.7 to 5.9 range. To help avoid diversion to the Frightful Variation or the Blank, this route is given in somewhat greater than normal detail.

Begin in the alcove 15 feet left of the Blank and 30 feet left of the first pitch of the Angel's Fright. Climb a difficult 5.8 vertical jam crack to a small ledge. Continue straight up ten feet on slightly easier climbing and traverse left six feet. Again go straight up 15 feet past an expansion bolt to the belay ledge on the Frightful Variation of the Trough. Continue straight up on 4th class flakes to an open face where two more bolts can be used for protection. Small holds of steady 5.7 difficulty lead to a small overhang. Pass the overhang and traverse 15 feet right to reach a thin vertical crack. Ascend 15 feet to another bolt (5.9). Diagonal left and up past the bolt on easier climbing to reach the Swing Traverse. The top of the rock may be reached by numerous variations ranging from the Trough to the Angel's Fright.

35. THE BLANK   Class 5.10   5 hours

FA: May 1954; D. Wilson, R. Robbins, J. Gallwas

For many years the Blank was an aid climb. The first free ascent was made in 1960 by T. Frost and R. Kamps. About 20 feet left of the first pitch of the Angel's Fright (Route 39) ascend a thin crack to Litter Ledge. Climb directly up past an overhang to an unseen belay ledge about 70 feet above. This overhang is straight-forward if ascended with aid, but is very difficult as a free pitch. Direct progress from this ledge is blocked by a dark overhang which provides a possible though unprotected 5th class jam crack to the next ledge 30 feet above. The usual route traverses left a short distance to shallow thin direct aid cracks which lead straight up 40 feet to a small overhang. Traverse back to the right, eventually working up to a bush on a sloping ledge. From this bush, the easiest line is to move right, climb up and then move back left to a difficult lieback crack. Above is a delicate traverse left across a smooth face, protected by a bolt. Beyond this point easier climbing leads directly to the Swing Traverse (Route 38) which can be followed left to Pine Tree Ledge of the Trough or right to Lunch Ledge on the Angel's Fright. Twelve to twenty chocks or pitons depending on the extent of direct aid.

36. JONAH   Class 5.10+   6 hours

FA: August 1964; T. Higgins, R. Coats, M. Cohen

Though there is hardly room for another route between the Blank and the Angel's Fright, this route is quite distinct from both of these. It is unusual because of the sustained nature of the climbing, every pitch involving some 5.10 climbing. Start in the middle of the small face between the Blank and the Angel's Fright. The short pitch to Litter Ledge is 5.9 or possibly 5.10 in difficulty. Now ascend the slightly overhanging headwall above, keeping in and under a short dihedral that arches to the right (5.10). From a small platform at the end of the arch, undercling left beneath a roof and climb straight up to a bushy ledge. The next pitch zigzags to another bushy ledge (5.9), the initial move being difficult and unprotected. Above this ledge, two expansion anchors protect a delicate mantle and short traverse right (5.9) to a crack which leads to the Whale's Mouth, a prominent roofed cavity (also known to some climbers as the "Ubangi Lips"). Awkward chimney climbing (5.7) in the Whale's Mouth leads to Lunch Ledge, and a short pitch directly overhead leads to a smaller ledge. The summit pitch starts with an awkward mantle and extreme edging (5.10+) which leads to a bolt and easier (5.9) friction up a smooth unbroken mass of rock on the West Shoulder.

37. FRIGHTFUL VARIATION OF THE TROUGH
Class 5.2   2 hours

FA: September 1944; C. Wilts, J. Gorin

Ascend the first short chimney pitch of the Angel's Fright (Route 39) to Litter Ledge. Cross left and ascend the deep crack at the right edge of a large exfoliation slab to a small belay ledge. From the left end of the ledge, continue up and left on a rather obvious route to join the Trough at Pine

Tree Ledge. At one or two points a chock may be found
advisable.

38. SWING TRAVERSE   Class 5.1   30 minutes

FA: Unknown

The Swing Traverse is a convenient way of crossing the
West Face between routes near the Trough and those near
the Angel's Fright or Fingertip. From right to left, start at
Lunch Ledge (see Route 39) and continue left along the
ledge until it narrows and breaks off. A good belay stance
protects the leader in the following traverse. Climb out onto
the face and down a left facing lieback onto some solution
ledges awkwardly below the end of the crack. Traverse to
the left on small footholds, climbing slightly to reach Pine
Tree Ledge on the Trough.

   In the opposite direction there is no close belay stance.
It is best to climb up above the traverse and climb out right
to snap into a fixed pin. This gives good protection even
with the belayer far back to the left.

39. ANGEL'S FRIGHT   Class 5.4   3 hours

FA: September 1936; J. Smith, W. Rice

The name of the Angel's Fright will be recognized by the
older Los Angeles residents as a derivation from the name
of the cable car route "Angel's Flight," a typical Bob Brinton pun. The route follows the prominent shallow trough
above Lunch Rock. The route starts in a narrow chimney
with small chockstones about 100 feet left from a point di-

rectly above Lunch Rock. At the top of the chimney is Litter Ledge, a broad ledge with a large fir tree. The Frightful Variation of the Trough (Route 37) leaves at this point. From the tree ascend 80 feet, finally traversing right to a broad belay ledge. The easiest route on this pitch makes use of the face to the right of the main crack, and returning to the main crack via the "Letterbox" foothold. Above, 4th class climbing leads up a V trough to a slight overhang which is the last difficulty of the ascent. Twenty feet above this spot is Lunch Ledge, a six-foot shelf just above a small yellow pine, where the Fingertrip, Fingertip, Fingergrip, Switchbacks, Blanketty-Blank, Human Fright, and Frightful Fright come in from the right, and the Swing Traverse comes in from the left.

Several 4th or 5th class routes can be followed to the West Shoulder. The usual route ascends large three-foot steps on the left and then bears right over bushes to a very marked trough leading farther right to a short easy overhang and the west end of the West Shoulder. Several variations to the left of the trough offer more difficult and more interesting friction and lieback pitches to the West Shoulder. Three or four chocks are adequate.

40. FRIGHTFUL FRIGHT   Class 5.11   5 hours

FA: July 1953; R. Robbins, D. Wilson

This route lies on the narrow buttress between the Angel's Fright and the Human Fright. Since it shares belay ledges with both of these routes, many interconnections are possible. For 25 years, the first pitch was climbed free (5.9), and the last two pitches to Lunch Ledge were climbed with aid (A2). In 1978, these pitches were climbed free by J. Long and M. Leclinski, the last pitch rather unprotected 5.10 and the middle pitch reaching 5.11 in difficulty.

The first 40 feet are deceptively difficult. The face seems well broken by cracks, but is clearly 5.9 in difficulty. Above the climbing eases until an awkward 5.9 move around a corner to the right blocks progress to the first belay ledge. The second pitch starts with 5.11 face climbing to reach a vertical crack which is followed 50 feet. Move left and up past a fixed pin to the next belay ledge. Above, difficult and currently unprotected face climbing (5.10) is followed by easier moves to a bolt and beyond to Lunch Ledge. Take plenty of chocks including several very thin ones.

41. HUMAN FRIGHT   Class 5.10   4 hours

FA: June 1952; J. Mendenhall, R. Robbins

This route is often climbed using direct aid. The first free ascent was made by R. Kamps. The route is parallel to and about 30 feet right of the Angel's Fright. It follows a deep right-facing right-angled crack which eventually becomes an overhanging arch extending right to meet the opposite arch of the Fingertrip (Route 45). The route though difficult is obvious so little route description is necessary. Near the end of the arch, ascend to the ledge just above. Climb the face diagonally up and right to reach the Fingertip ledge just below Lunch Ledge. As many as ten or 20 chocks may be used, depending on the extent of direct aid used.

42. SWITCHBACKS   Class 5.8   3 hours

FA: July 1953; J. Gallwas, B. Lilley

Just right of the Human Fright ascend the nearly vertical face about 15 feet and traverse right to a small scrub oak on an equally small ledge. The route traverses 10 feet right from this point on very improbable looking footholds then proceeds up to a good belay ledge. From the far left end of the ledge, ascend a block and traverse left. Then climb straight up and traverse back right. This traverse involves an awkward spread eagle and the leader must take care to provide adequate protection for the last man on the rope. The traverse continues right and joins the Fingertrip at the beginning of the overhanging arch.

An interesting variation at the beginning of the climb starts about 50 feet right and ascends directly to the first belay ledge. An expansion anchor is used for protection on this class 5.7 pitch.

43. BLANKETTY-BLANK   Class 5.10   4 hours

FA: June 1959; T. Frost, H. Daley

Blanker than the Blank was the consensus of the first ascent party. Aid was used at several points. The first free ascent was made in 1963 by R. Kamps and T. Higgins. The route is not well defined by natural features, but the following description may be of some help. The start is on a very improbable blank face about 100 feet right and downhill from the Switchbacks. Climb the face to a horizontal crack under a small arch and traverse right to a small bush. Ascend the face above on small holds to a belay spot about 80 feet from the base. Ascend an easy crack for 30 feet to a small ledge above which is a very blank area. Here a knifeblade piton driven straight up under a flake was used for direct aid on the early ascents. The flake has since come off and protection is now provided by a sound expansion bolt. With the more secure protection, the climb is now often made without aid. On reaching the ledge on which the Switchbacks finally traverses right to the Fingertrip, traverse left 25 feet. Climb up on small holds to a small ledge where two bolts can be used to establish a belay.

Various routes are possible on the smooth face above. The preferred route goes straight up 50 or 60 feet from the belay ledge to the apex of the Human Fright and Fingertrip arches. One bolt is available to protect the more difficult 5.10 moves.

44. THE SLAB   Class 5.8   3 hours

FA: August 1958; H. Daley, D. McClelland

A prominent exfoliation slab about 200 feet high borders the right side of the smooth face containing the Switchbacks (Route 42) and the Blanketty-Blank (Route 43). This route follows the wide crack beneath and on the left side of the slab to its upper section where a dog-leg crack leads upward across the face of the slab. The route ends at the top of the slab where an easy traverse leads to the early pitches of the Fingertrip. This was originally climbed with direct aid. The first free ascent was made in 1963 by R Kamps and TM Herbert.

45. FINGERTRIP   Class 5.7   4 hours

FA: September 1946; C. Wilts, D. Gillespie, J. Rosenblatt

The traverse of the Fingertip lies just above a prominent

arch which sweeps up and left to join the Human Fright arch coming up from the left. The Fingertrip runs parallel to the Fingertip under the overhanging arch. Progress is largely through use of lieback cracks which give the route its name. The arch can be reached in several ways, but the recommended approach is given below.

Just right of the Slab is a shallow red-stained trough which is ascended for 150 feet to a fir tree growing on a ledge. Where progress to the tree is blocked, ascend a narrow crack which leads diagonally up and left on the smooth face. Traverse back to the fir tree ledge. Above ascend a short difficult jam crack to 4th class scrambling. This point may also be reached by a short traverse from the Fingertip or by one or two variations in between. Proceed upward for about 40 feet and then traverse left, turning a corner which leads under the prominent arching formation below the Fingertip Traverse. At the end of the arch where it is joined by the Human Fright arch, climb over a slight overhang and continue up over easy rock to Lunch Ledge. Easily protected by chocks and a fixed pin.

46. FINGERTIP TRAVERSE   Class 5.3   3 hours

FA: Setember 1936; J. Smith, R. Brinton, A. Johnson,
   W. Rice

The Fingertip Traverse, more commonly called simply the Fingertip, has been long considered the ideal classic climb for the serious beginner. From Lunch Rock follow the trail to the right to the west end of the rock. Just short of the West Buttress, four trees stand close together. The first and fourth are large sugar pines and the middle ones are small firs. Just above to the left is found a gully or broad trough containing at its lower end a line of shrubs or small trees (mostly mountain mahogany) and at its upper end a large pine tree under an overhang. Ascend the gully to this point. Climb the tree to an upper branch from which one can climb out left around the corner of the overhang onto the edge of the ridge. Ascend easy rock and bushes to the highest bush or shrub-tree. The next pitch includes a short classical lieback. From the top of this pitch traverse left to the Fingertip Traverse. This follows a narrow ledge across the top of the overhanging arch of the Fingertrip. Halfway across, a sling around a stunted tree offers additional protection. From the end of the ledge continue diagonally up and left over sloping ledges to the broad six-foot Lunch Ledge. Here the Fingertip joins several other routes including the Angel's Fright and continues as described there. Two or three chocks will be needed in addition to the fixed pin at the start of the traverse.

VARIATION—THE TOETIP

It is possible to find variations which follow none of the regular pitches of any of the three Finger climbs lying between the Fingertrip and Fingertip to the start of the Fingertip Traverse, and between the Fingertip and Fingergrip above this point. M. and B. Powell reported their first ascent in 1966 did not exceed 5.8 in difficulty, but most climbers since that time have insisted that it is more difficult.

47. FINGERGRIP   Class 5.7   4 hours

FA: June 1947; R. Van Aken, I. Weeks, C. Kreiser

The fingergrip follows the first two or three pitches of the Fingertip (Route 46) and departs from it at the end of the

87

lieback pitch. The route then follows the deep crack which can be seen to the right and above this point. From the end of the lieback pitch ascend a thin crack straight up until climbing becomes very difficult. Make a delicate crossing to the right to the deep crack and continue up to a shallow cave. Traverse left under the overhanging roof of the cave and continue up the crack. The crack can be ascended as a difficult lieback or the most difficult part can be bypassed by a detour right, up, and back left to the crack. In any case, protection is difficult without large chocks. Near the end of the crack, traverse left across the face to Lunch Ledge. Instead of traversing left to Lunch Ledge, it is possible to traverse right on delicate friction and poor handholds around a corner (class 5.5). This connects the Fingergrip with Jensen's Jaunt and is sometimes called the Footslip Variation.

48. ANGLE IRON TRAVERSE   Class 5.7   3 hours

FA: July 1948; R. Van Aken, G. Harr

This route has two approaches. The best is from a point near the top of the lieback pitch on the Fingertip (Route 46). Cross right and ascend the wall on the right at a low spot. This maneuver is quite difficult but is well protected. Follow an obvious crack diagonally right to a large block providing an excellent belay. On the route of first ascent this block was reached by a short rope traverse left from the difficult corner of Jensen's Jaunt (Route 51). This traverse has also been accomplished as a difficult free lead.

From this block the "traverse" starts, following cracks up and left past some small bushes. These cracks end at the

Footslip Ledge which may be followed right to the upper part of Jensen's Jaunt or left to the upper part of the Fingergrip.

49. EL CAMINO REAL   Class 5.10   6 hours

FA: November 1961; R. Robbins, H. Daley, J. Taylor

The first part of El Camino Real lies on the narrow face between the Fingertip (Route 46) and the Traitor Horn group (Routes 51 to 53). About 30 feet right of the Fingertip and near a prominent sugar pine, ascend a smooth face just left of a slight crack for 25 feet. Move left around a small overhang and ascend 30 feet to a smooth face. A horn of rock sits on the right at the base of this face. The next two pitches are the most challenging. Some broken rock on the right provides access to small holds and a thin shallow crack is followed upward. Diagonal left 20 or 30 feet to a small jungle of scrub trees (mostly mountain mahogany). The lieback pitch of the fingertip starts at the left of this jungle. Another incomparably more difficult starts at the right of the jungle. It is possible that the leader may want to descend to rest after placing protection if there are no fixed pins in place. The lieback crack is long and instead of improving, deteriorates near the top.

At the top of this pitch, the Angle Iron Traverse crosses from the Fingertip and continues right over the vertical wall forming the lieback. Continue up the lieback crack joining the Fingergrip at the end of its first pitch. Many leaders will be more comfortable carrying a few pitons on this route.

50. THE HANGOVER   Class 5.12   4 hours

FA: August 1954; R. Robbins, J. Gallwas, F. Martin,
     M. Sherrick

The West Buttress is topped by a large overhanging block.
Jensen's Jaunt passes it on the left, and the Traitor Horn
passes it on the right. The ultimate objective of the Hangover is to directly ascend the overhang. This challenging
overhang was long thought to be one of the direct aid problems that would never succumb to a free ascent, but even
this route has now been climbed free by J. Long in 1978.

The Hangover may be reached by ascending the first
two pitches of the Traitor Horn, but a more interesting alternative is a smaller gully to the left of this route. From the
first horn of the Traitor Horn route, thin cracks lead circui-
tously up the overhang above, first to a small ledge covered
with guano and then left and up. The last usual direct aid
piton is behind a small insecure flake. The free move is
slightly to the right, protected by a bolt and fixed pin. After
the strenuous pull-up over the lip of the overhang, easy
though steep friction leads to the lower end of the West
Shoulder.

51. JENSEN'S JAUNT   Class 5.6   2 hours

FA: August 1938; C. Jensen, J. Smith, D. MacDonald

Jensen's Jaunt is a variation or alternate to the difficult pitch
on the Traitor Horn. It is rumored that it was first used as a
route to the top following a fall off of the horn. The variation starts at the base of the huge block overhanging the upper part of the West Buttress. Instead of traversing to the

right onto the Traitor Horn, continue to the left around the north corner of the block, along steep sloping slabs at its base. Continue for one or two pitches until it is possible to climb up to the right onto the top of the block, joining the Traitor Horn route on the steep friction pitches above the second or true horn. An alternate to these relatively un-protected friction pitches is to cross a smooth face on the left on small friction holds to easier pitches just below the West Shoulder.

52. TRAITOR HORN   Class 5.8   4 hours

FA: August 1938; J. Smith, A. Johnson, M. Holton

This climb was an early favorite at Tahquitz. Originally climbed with aid, the first free ascent was made by R. Gorin and W. Shand about 1941. The route begins at the western-most end of the rock to the left of the sharp edge of the West Buttress. A prominent landmark on this route is a sharp horn which can be seen from several points along the base of the rock, jutting out high on the buttress. Ascend first over steep ledges and slabs to the lower end of a deep crack or dihedral which leads to the left base of the huge block overhanging the upper part of the buttress. At the base of the block traverse to the right along a narrow crack onto a point of rock jutting from the base of the buttress block. This proves not to be the horn described earlier, hence the name, Traitor Horn. From here the second or true horn is visible above and to the right. Continue the tra-verse to a small platform below and to the left of an alcove below the horn. From the platform climb ten feet straight up in the angle of the alcove, and cross the smooth exposed face to the base of the horn. A narrow ledge at the level at the top of the horn enables one to swing out and straddle the horn. Stand up and with some difficulty climb onto the ridge above. Steep unprotected slabs lead to the west end of the West Shoulder. It is also possible to ascend the horn using the deep crack just to its left.

53. LAST JUDGMENT

LOWER SECTION   **Class 5.11   4 hours**

FA: September 1964; T. Higgins, I. Couch

This route has slowly evolved over the years, and in view of recent activity on the edge of the West Buttress it would appear that the final book has not yet been written for this climb. Start in a dihedral about 20 feet right of the Traitor Horn route. Continue over a loose overhang and up on small holds until further progress becomes improbable. Traverse left to a belay tree on the Horn route. On the second pitch cross right on potholes past two expansion bolts. Sharp flakes lead up and right to a third bolt. Very difficult (5.11) climbing to the left and up leads to an obvious bush. From the bush climb directly up into the alcove of the Traitor Horn. The first free ascent of the most difficult pitch was made in 1976 or 1977 by F. Ziel, E. Ericson and F. Noble.

UPPER SECTION–THE PEARLY GATE   Class 5.9

FA: D. Rearick, R. Kamps

The Pearly Gate is the obvious appropriate climax to the

Last Judgment, although continuous consecutive ascents of the two routes are rare. From the small platform at the left side of the alcove of the Traitor Horn, climb straight up the left angle of the alcove. Near the top, the crack becomes a severe overhanging lieback, with protection difficult for the last ten feet.

THE SOUTH FACE

ROUTES 54–83

To the right of the West Buttress the height of the rock diminishes, but the angle increases. The Unchaste, the Chauvinist, and the Ski Tracks (Route 63) in the middle of this face have the highest average angle of any major routes on the rock. The photograph of the South Face shows most of the routes between the Open Book (Route 54) and the X-Crack (Route 69).

Just right of the West Buttress is a deep right angle formed by two nearly vertical faces of rock. The crack in the bottom of this angle is the Open Book. About 20 feet to the right are the cracks which form the Mechanic's Route (Route 56). A few feet farther right is the Green Arch (Route 57). This arch, or rather half arch, is just left of the large tree in the photograph of the South Face. In the middle of the sheer face, the Ski Tracks proceed up two parallel cracks. A couple of hundred feet to the right (at the extreme right of the photograph) is the prominent X of the X-Crack. Five very challenging routes are found between the Ski Tracks and the X-Crack.

Beyond the X-Crack, the height of the rock continually diminishes. Fourteen more routes are found between this point and the Notches. Although these are short climbs, many of them are exceedingly difficult. The principal exception is the Friction Route which provides an easy 3rd class route for descending from the West Shoulder.

54. OPEN BOOK   Class 5.9   4 hours

FA: September 1947; J. Mendenhall, H. Sutherland

On the right flank of the West Buttress, a great right angle is formed by two nearly vertical faces of rock. The Open Book follows this dihedral for two or three pitches. The first pitch starts ten feet right of the crack and ascends a slight overhang to a ledge eight feet above the base. Traverse left to the Open Book crack and climb directly up. The class 5.9 section is up a vertical jam crack on the left side of the dihedral to a large flake on the right side that can be seen from the bottom.

The next pitch consists of an 80-foot crack about three inches wide. On the original ascent, 2×4 wood pitons were placed; the last of these was removed on the third ascent. The crack may be climbed by lieback or jamming. The latter seems somewhat safer, but proves to be also more strenuous. Protection is not easy, but wide chocks and a sling on a flake are adequate. The Open Book crack ends in a "cave with no bottom." The exit from this cave to the right is the last difficulty of the ascent. Another pitch in a chimney ends

on the West Shoulder. The first free ascent of this route was
made by R. Robbins and D. Wilson.

55. ZIGZAG   Class 5.10   4 hours

FA: TM Herbert, M. Powell

This route lies in a zigzag pattern on the narrow face between the Open Book and the Mechanic's Route. Except at
the start and finish, the climber need not touch these
routes. The first free ascent was achieved by M. Powell and
R. Kamps in 1967. Start midway between the Open Book
and Green Arch. Ascend a few feet and then move left and
up to an expansion bolt. Climb straight up (5.8), crossing
the Mechanic's Route where it traverses right from the
Open Book. Continue up a prominent and strenuous lieback crack which lies five or ten feet left of the Mechanic's
Route. Above where this crack merges with the Mechanic's
Route, zig to the left over a small overhanging horn. Above
this is the most difficult pitch (5.10). Join the Mechanic's
Route on the right or the Open Book on the left for the last
pitch to the top of the West Shoulder.

56. MECHANIC'S ROUTE   Class 5.8   4 hours

FA: October 1937; G. Dawson, R. Jones

The first portion of this route follows the Open Book. After
climbing about 40 feet, make a delicate traverse across the
face 20 feet to the right. This is best protected by ascending
the Open Book a few feet farther to use a fixed pin or chock
to protect the traverse. The ascent continues straight up a

second deep crack. Where the crack narrows and progress becomes very difficult, solution depressions will be found dotting the steep massive face to the right. The lead to the right, up, and back over the solution ledges is not difficult, but the exposure is great. On about the sixth ascent an expansion anchor was driven to provide protection near the top of this pitch. A short distance above, the crack may be left using an interesting traverse right to an easy chimney ending at the West Shoulder. The usual route leads directly up over one delicate point to the top.

57. THE GREEN ARCH
Class 5.8 & A2 or 5.11   4 hours

FA: May 1953; D. Wilson, R. Smith

This route is Tahquitz' best for training in aid climbing. For years there was no concern about free ascents since if nothing else, protection would be all but impossible. Nevertheless a free ascent was accomplished in 1975 by J. Long and T. Sorenson. It is exceptionally strenuous when climbed in this way.

Immediately to the right of the Mechanic's Route, an exfoliating slab has fallen away, forming a long right angle crack extending first up and then arching slightly to the right. Green lichen is prominent on the upper part of the arch, hence the name, but the name is really a misnomer since the crack forms only a rudimentary beginning of an arch. Two variations lead to the base of the main crack. One starts at the overhang about 20 feet right of the Open Book crack, the other is ten or 15 feet farther right. Since protection is poor on the right crack, many climbers prefer to climb it with direct aid.

When ascended with aid, the main crack itself is easy A1 climbing except near the top where it reaches A2 in difficulty. From the last fixed pin under the overhang on the right, it is possible to step right onto a small foothold on the open face above the crack. Continue up 50 feet on small holds using three expansion bolts for protection. Easy class 4 climbing leads to the West Shoulder.

VARIATION

From a point below the top of the arch it is possible to swing left around the lip of the arch, reaching a ledge which leads to the Mechanic's Route a short distance below the solution pits. This was the route of first ascent by Wilson and Smith in 1953. The more interesting ending described earlier was discovered by M. and B. Powell eleven years later.

58. FLYING CIRCUS   Class 5.11 & A4   5 hours

FA: August 1978; R. Accomazzo, R. Muir

An improbable rock face is found between the Green Arch and the Unchaste. Climb the face to a thin lieback crack (5.10) which is followed until the wall is severely overhanging. Aid climbing (A4) with rurps and hooks gains a bolt which protects 20 feet of 5.11 face climbing to belay bolts. Easier face climbing (5.10+) continues past two bolts.

59. THE UNCHASTE
Class 5.9 & A3 or 5.10+   5 hours

FA: September 1957; R. Robbins, M. Sherrick

99

This route starts from the left side of a broad cave below and to the left of the Ski Tracks (Route 63). A short free lead up and to the right brings one to a direct aid crack running back to the left below a small overhang. Above the end of this crack there is an expansion bolt from which a small ledge can be reached. A difficult mantle followed by some delicate climbing leads to a gully where a good belay can be established. In 1974, T. Sorenson and G. Lewis found a very difficult free ascent, traversing left on the face just above the overhang. It is protected by bolts, but is so difficult that even clipping in protection is tricky.

From the lower end of the belay gully, the route traverses left on small holds and then follows two vertical cracks to a shallow bowl below a second bolt. A difficult traverse right leads to a third bolt and 60 feet of open face climbing.

VARIATION

This variation by M. and B. Powell replaces the upper pitches with an easier alternative. From the second bolt, it runs diagonally left to join the Green Arch near the top.

60. THE OFFSHOOT   Class 5.8   2 hours

FA: January 1964; M. Powell, T. Rygg, R. Coats

Near the left end of the first ledge of the Sling Swing Traverse (Route 62) a series of small sloping ledges lead up and to the left. Two expansion anchors (one at the start of the route) protect the most difficult moves. Above the second bolt, class 3 climbing leads to the top of the West Shoulder. Delightful friction and interesting route finding make this an enjoyable alternate to the upper part of the Ski Tracks.

61. THE CHAUVINIST   Class 5.7   3 hours

FA: January 1964; M. Powell, T. Rygg, R. Coats

The Chauvinist parallels the Ski Tracks very closely, but the climber need not actually touch the latter route except possibly for protecting the leader. Start at the very bottom of the left Ski Track and ascend 30 feet passing through a slightly overhanging chimney. Above, traverse left a few feet to avoid the regular Ski Track route and climb the open face about 100 feet to a belay ledge where the Sling Swing Traverse begins. With a short climbing rope it may be necessary to move over to the Ski Tracks to find a closer belay stance.

Above the Sling Swing ledge, interesting open face climbing continues straight up about 100 feet (while the Ski Tracks veer slightly right). Three expansion anchors will be found to protect the most difficult parts of this pitch. Above, easy 4th class climbing leads to the West Shoulder.

62. SLING SWING TRAVERSE   Class 5.9

FA: September 1951; C. & E. Wilts, J. Moore

This traverse halfway up the South Face provides access between routes near the Ski Tracks and those near the Mechanic's Route. The first ascent was from right to left. The first free ascents in both directions were made by M. Powell. *w/T. RYGG belaying*

From a point halfway up the principal cracks of the Ski Tracks, traverse left on a small ledge to its end. Ascend two or three feet to a small shelf. An expansion anchor here gives good protection for the two delicate steps to easier climbing.

In the reverse direction, traverse right from the Mechanic's Route on delicate but easy friction. Where climbing becomes difficult there are no cracks or expansion bolts. By climbing up on a small ledge it is possible to put a sling around a small rock knob some ten feet above the traverse. The route in this direction is distinctly more difficult and is rated 5.10.

63. THE SKI TRACKS   Class 5.5   3 hours

FA: September 1947; C. Wilts, R. Van Aken

The Ski Tracks are a pair of nearly vertical cracks in the middle of the South Face of Tahquitz Rock. The two cracks are separated by about ten feet over their entire length. From the base of the rock, ascend to a broad platform leading to the base of the cracks. The first one or two pitches are on the nearly vertical face between the cracks on unbelievably good holds (causing one climber to describe it as 3rd class climbing on a vertical face). Above, the route follows the left crack to its end. At this point four alternates are possible to finish the ascent.

a. Standard route: A delicate step around a corner to the right leads to the first of three platforms on the otherwise sheer face. Proceed to the third platform. A steep awkward chute leads up to the right 15 feet to a fourth platform, where Routes 65 to 68 (Chingadera to Innominate) join this route. Ascend an eight-foot vertical face on the left and traverse left 100 feet on a narrow 4th class ledge, to the top of the West Buttress.

b. A more interesting variation on the last pitch departs from the fourth platform, ascending a prominent crack on the right until it ends. A delicate, poorly protected 15-foot traverse to the right leads to easy scrambling. (C. & E. Wilts)

c. From the first and second platforms there are various possibilities on the broken face above (instead of traversing to the third platform). These are not as strenuous as (a) and easier than (b).

d. The most interesting variation starts at the end of the left Ski Track. Instead of turning the corner to the right, climb up and left across a very smooth face (one expansion bolt for protection) to a broken area and easier climbing. This variation is class 5.9 in difficulty. (R. Kamps, C. Wilts, M. & B. Powell)

64. RIGHT SKI TRACK   Class 5.8   4 hours

FA: September 1957; G. Harr, W. Dixon

This splendid variation of the Ski Tracks ascends the right crack of the Ski Tracks. Climbing difficulty is about 5.7 up to the end of the crack. Using an anchor for protection, descend about ten feet and make a delicate traverse across the face to the right. Follow a crack up and back left to a small black chimney, which is the most strenuous part of the climb. Immediately above this chimney is the first of the three platforms described in Route 63. Follow any of the variations to the summit.

VARIATION

From the top of the right Ski Track, ascend the face to the left using an expansion bolt for protection to join the regular Ski Track route just before the Steparound. This was the route of first ascent used by G. Harr and W. Dixon in September 1957. However, the route described above is more challenging and interesting. It was first ascended by D. Rearick, M. and B. Powell.

103

65. CHINGADERA   Class 5.11   4 hours

FA: February 1967; R. Kamps, M. Powell

Midway between the Ski Tracks and the Reach, ascend a vertical crack for 25 feet to its end. A delicate step up to the first expansion anchor starts 50 feet of sustained difficult face climbing with no piton cracks. The eight expansion anchors can be passed without using direct aid although several moves from the fifth to the seventh anchor are very difficult (class 5.10+). At the fifth bolt traverse up and left six feet to a sixth anchor, then traverse directly left about eight feet on a slightly projecting rounded rib to the seventh bolt. Above the climbing no longer exceeds class 5.9 in difficulty. Ten feet up pass the eighth bolt which protects a 5.9 move to easier ground. From this point it is possible to move right to the belay ledge of the Black Harlot's Layaway, or one can continue straight up a short distance. An awkward step to the right leads to a diagonal hand traverse up and to the right to the ledge where the Innominate and Reach join the Ski Tracks.

On the first ascent of this face (April 1964), M. Powell and S. Altman climbed the lower part of this route and the upper part of Route 66. The connection was made by a traverse from the fifth bolt to the right past another anchor to join the Black Harlot's Layaway.

66. BLACK HARLOT'S LAYAWAY
Class 5.11   3 hours

FA: September 1968; M. & B. Powell, R. Kamps

The Layaway starts in the 4th class gully which forms the

first pitch of the Reach. About ten or 20 feet before the first "reach," traverse left and up onto the face past an expansion anchor (class 5.9). Continue up and left past two more bolts to a difficult crack which is followed up and left to a good belay ledge. One additional anchor will be found on this section. Most climbers make an easy tension traverse on this bolt. In 1974, T. Sorenson, J. Bachar and G. Lewis were able to bypass this aid using 5.11 moves on the face about ten feet below the bolt. Above the belay ledge, 15 feet of easy climbing is followed by a short class 5.8 jam crack which leads to the diagonal hand traverse at the top of the Chingadera.

67. THE REACH   Class 5.8 & A1   or 5.11+

FA: September 1956; M. Sherrick, R. Robbins

To the left of the corner forming the Innominate there is a class 4 gully slanting diagonally upward to the right joining the Innominate at the base of the double overhang. The Reach starts in and follows this gully for about two-thirds of its length, then traverses the face to the left (the first "reach") to a ledge. Three expansion anchors (A1) have been placed on the smooth face above this ledge. The free move (the second "reach") from the top bolt is the most interesting and difficult maneuver on the climb. Above this point there are two alternatives. The route of first ascent proceeds directly up using several pitons for direct aid followed by enjoyable face climbing. An alternate route requiring no aid was found by M. and B. Powell. Where climbing in the crack becomes very difficult, traverse right around the corner and ascend the face using a bolt for protection. Eventually traverse back left to the original route.

This was reported to be 5.8 in difficulty, though several climbers have found it to be more like 5.9.

The smooth vertical face between the two reaches was believed to be beyond the reach of free climbing, but new generation climbers have found some very tenuous holds to the left of the bolts. The first free ascent was made by J. Long, E. Eriksson, and R. Accomazzo in 1978. Tentative rating is severe 5.11. Fortunately bolts are nearby to protect the nearly inevitable falls.

68. THE INNOMINATE   Class 5.9   3 hours

FA: August 1947; C. Wilts, G. Bloom

The Innominate ascends the double overhang at the deep niche in the South Face about 150 yards right of the Ski Tracks. It is approached from the right by an easy traverse followed by 40 feet of climbing, including a very difficult jam crack to the top of a block directly beneath the over-hang. The next pitch resembles a miniature Open Book with both leaves of the book overhanging. On the first as-cent, pitons were used for direct aid over the overhang. It was first climbed free by R. Robbins and J. Gallwas. Above this pitch, the route joins the Ski Tracks.

The block beneath the overhang may also be reached from the left by an interesting direct aid variation (R. Rob-bins, M. Sherrick)

69. X-CRACK   Class 5.7 & A4   3 hours

FA: February 1965; M. Powell, F. DeSaussure,
    G. Hemming

Follow the easy traverse at the beginning of the Innominate to its end. On the overhanging face on the right is found a large X formed by two intersecting cracks. Follow the lower right branch of the X to the center (class A3). At this point it is very difficult to continue up the upper right branch which ultimately becomes the central part of the route. Instead continue past the center, ascending the left upper branch a short distance until it is possible to traverse over to the right branch and easier climbing (A1). Farther up this branch, the climbing probably reaches class A4 in difficulty at two places. The final 40 feet of open face climbing is protected by two expansion bolts. It is unlikely that this route can be climbed using only chocks.

70. TM'S JEWEL　　　　Class 5.7 & A4　　　4 hours

FA: June 1965; M. Powell, D. Lauria

This route begins near the right hand edge of the over-hanging wall that forms the right flank of the Innominate. Climb diagonally left up a crack 20 feet past a dead bush where direct aid becomes desirable. After a few pitons, three direct aid anchors (plus an intervening rurp) lead to a shallow bottoming vertical crack. It is necessary to ascend about 30 feet up this crack with very difficult piton place-ment (class A3 to A4 sustained) before a reliable piton can be driven. The angle of the wall eases here (to merely verti-cal) for about ten feet after which an expansion anchor can be used to protect about 15 feet of class 5.7 open face climb-ing. Here the route joins the upper easier portions of the Orange Peel.

71. PAS DE DEUX   Class 5.10   3 hours

FA: May 1974; G. Lewis, T. Sorenson

For many years, the right angle buttress between TM's Jewel and Daley's Direct was the major unsolved climbing problem at Tahquitz. Rather surprisingly the route is only rated 5.10. Start at TM's Jewel or just to the right. The standup beneath the small overhang is particularly challenging. About five bolts will be found to mark the route. A few pitons and chocks were used in addition to the bolts.

VARIATION

Ten years earlier, a partial ascent had been accomplished by traversing left from about 20 feet up Daley's Direct. Two expansion bolts will be found to protect the traverse to the last bolt of the regular route. (T. Higgins, T. Cochrane)

72. DALEY'S DIRECT   Class 5.6   1 hour

FA: October 1959; Y. Chouinard, H. Daley

From the base of the Friction Route, traverse left on a broad bushy ledge below the Orange Peel. The ledge ends at a small stunted sugar pine 50 feet below the Orange Peel flake. From the tree ascend more or less directly up to a sloping ledge about ten feet below the Orange Peel. Traverse right and up, crossing the Orange Peel route and then continue straight up 20 feet past a bolt to a good belay ledge.

The second pitch is on massive granite with no cracks for chock placement. Ascend ten feet to a sloping "ledge" which leads up and left on high angle friction. Those worried about lack of protection on this pitch can traverse right to the Climb With No Beginning. Several climbers have suggested a lower classification for this route (5.5 or even 5.4), but I still hold to the 5.6 rating.

73. ORANGE PEEL   Class 5.5   1 hour

FA: 1951; C. Wilts, E. Wilts

Near the bottom of the Friction Route the low cliff to the left can be partially ascended by means of a block projecting out to the right. From this block traverse left on friction to the "Orange Peel" a prominent orange colored flake. From here a delicate step leads straight up to good footholds and easy 4th and 3rd class scrambling. Protection at the flake is poor and an expansion anchor is in place for those who feel the added protection is desirable.

74. BABY'S BUTT   Class5.5   1 hour

FA: March 1960; Y. Chouinard and others

Start ten feet left of the Climb With No Beginning and climb up on the characteristic white area which gives the route its name. Continue diagonally up and left to a red solution hole where an angle piton can be easily driven. Continue straight up 20 feet to a thin crack. This crack does not take chocks well and due to overuse does not accept pitons. The climbing is not difficult at any point above the initial move, but the high exposure may justify placement of an expansion bolt.

75. CLIMB WITH NO BEGINNING
Class 5.6   ½ hour

FA: May 1950; C. Wilts, R. Cosgrove, G. Harr,
    R. Van Aken

The Climb With No beginning is the central route crossing
the short vertical wall which flanks the left side of the Friction Route gullies. About 100 feet right of the Orange Peel
a small but prominent gully can be seen up on the side of
the South Face. The route derives its name from the fact
that the lower end of the gully is just out of reach above a
rather smooth part of the short vertical wall mentioned
above. The route crosses the wall at a small slanting overhang. Ten feet above a vertical hole will be found in which
an angle piton can be dropped. Though loose, it gives adequate protection for the one or two delicate steps above.
The gully itself is class 3.

76. DIDDLY   Class 5.10   2 hours

FA: January 1967; M. Powell, R. Kamps

Midway between the Climb With No Beginning and the Liz-
ard's Leap, the Diddly follows a nearly direct route up the
smooth crackless face. Detailed description is unnecessary
since the route is well marked by the six expansion anchors
placed for protection. The climb involves difficult friction,
edging and fingernail holds. Difficulty is sustained class 5.7
except for one move at the halfway point which is probably
class 5.10. No need to carry any hardware except carabiners.

77. LIZARD'S LEAP   Class 5.9   2 hours

FA: November 1961; R. Robbins, H. Daley

A short distance right of the Climb With No Beginning and just left of the start of Fitschen's Folly there is a small white overhang with a crack running diagonally upward to the right. Climb directly over the overhang to a ledge where an expansion anchor will be found. Continue up on very delicate friction to a one-foot ledge. At the right end of this ledge a sling can be looped through a hole in the rock to provide further protection. The route continues up on smooth massive rock for about 50 or 60 feet to the end of roped climbing. Although this part is easier (class 5.6), the lack of protection is troublesome. Another bolt should be driven.

78. FITSCHEN'S FOLLY   Class 5.6   1 hour

First Descent: 1950; solo by J. Fitschen in one catastrophic
    uncontrolled fall.
FA: December 1954; D. Wilson, M. Powell

This route commemorates Joe Fitschen's 170-foot fall from the slabs above the Friction Route. Ascend the left (west) gully of the Friction Route and at a point 40 to 50 feet beyond the Climb With No Beginning work left to the ten-foot vertical wall which flanks the gully on the west. A small but prominent vertical crack will be found where a single chock may be used to protect the most difficult portion of the route. To aid in finding this spot, the climber should look for a large block wedged beneath a small overhanging arch. The starting point is about five feet left of this block. Ascend diagonally left on small holds to a small ledge above the steep wall. Climb back right and up to a good belay ledge.

If one wishes to finish this route the way Fitschen started it, it is necessary to make a traverse left across the middle of the upper smooth face instead of walking diagonally right to the Friction Route. This traverse is poorly protected and may exceed 5.7 in difficulty, but it is a much more exciting ending.

79. FRICTION ROUTE   Class 3   ½ hour

FA: 1936; J. Smith, M.J. Edwards

This route skirts the base of the steep South Face and reaches the West Shoulder from less steep rock to the southeast. As the name implies, it has mainly steep friction pitches which, for experienced climbers, require no roped climbing. The route is used primarily as a means of descent.

From a point about halfway to the Notches from the bottom of the West Buttress, two shallow troughs ascend diagonally right along the base of steeper cliffs. This point is marked by a large white fir growing about one foot from the bottom of the rock apron. Follow either of these routes, finally traversing left to two large pine trees standing together about halfway to the top of the Rock. Traverse farther left and up to the base of another face, then along ledges diagonally up to the right, emerging finally through a short chimney in a large block on the West Shoulder.

Since most interest in this route is as a quick method of descent, the following directions are given to locate the top of the route. From the west end of the West Shoulder (Routes 39 to 74) follow along the right (south) side of the ridge to two large boulders beside a dead tree and a large tree trunk in a clump of bushes. From the upper end of the West Shoulder (Routes 19 to 30) descend on the left (south) side of the ridge to the large boulders on the south edge of the shoulder. From the top of the largest (15-foot) boulder descend a chimney-like crack on the southeast side. Follow the route given above in reverse order, remembering that right and left in the description refers to a climber facing up the rock.

80. RED ROCK ROUTE   Class 5.1   ½ hour

FA: August 1953; D. Wilson, G. Hemming

From the Friction Route or from the West Shoulder of Tahquitz Rock, a red chimney can be seen leading up the summit block. Enter from the left and ascend to the summit in two easy pitches. At the belay stance it is possible to traverse right to more interesting variations.

81. THE BIG DADDY   Class 5.10   3 hours

FA: May 1959; Y. Chouinard, TM Herbert

Starting 30 feet right of the Red Rock Route, the initial difficulty on this route is an awkward step-around to the right on decomposed granite. Higher the route passes a very difficult overhang, and 20 feet higher crosses left to a prominent crack which is bordered by red stained rock,

113

particularly on the right. Here a belay may be set up. The second pitch proceeds directly upward to the summit over delicate friction.

Those attempting a free ascent on this route should take care to adequately protect the difficult overhang of the first pitch before making an all-out attempt on a route of this difficulty. The effort of placing protection without resorting to direct aid is particularly challenging. The first free ascent was made by T. Frost and R. Robbins.

82. THE LITTLE MOMMA   Class 5.10   2 hours

FA: 1961; C. Wilts, D. McClelland

This is a short route on the south buttress of the subsidiary (east) summit block. It is separated from the Big Daddy on the left by the deep cleft between the two summit blocks. An awkward difficult crack leads up from the bottom of the buttress to easier climbing. About halfway up, a short blank wall is ascended protected by a bolt. The first free ascent was made by J. Long in 1974.

83. UPSIDE DOWN CAKE   Class 5.10   2 hours

FA: July 1966; T. Higgins, R.Kamps

This one-pitch route follows the first prominent crack seen on walking down along the base of the South Face from the Notch. A five-foot roof is surprisingly moderate, but the final section of the crack is extremely awkward and strenuous. About six pitons including a 1½-inch, and some three- or four-inch angles may be helpful.

THE INNOMINATE
L. Reynolds

ON THE ROOF
OF LE TOIT

B. Turney

THE STEP-AROUND ON THE SKI TRACKS

Dolt

TRAITOR HORN
Dolt

HOODENETT
T. Frost

NORTH SIDE OF TAHQUITZ ROCK
B. Turney

WEST SIDE OF TAHQUITZ ROCK

B. Turney

SOUTH SIDE OF TAHQUITZ ROCK

EAST SIDE OF SUICIDE ROCK

L. Reynolds

END OF THE BAT
Dolt

END OF THE BAT
Dolt

THE CLIMBING ROUTES
ON
SUICIDE ROCK

THE SOUTHERN
BUTTRESSES AND FACES

ROUTES 1–14

The southernmost cliffs of Suicide Rock are little visited by climbers because of the lack of impressive faces when viewed from a distance and because most of the routes are short. However there are many opportunities for interesting climbing of all grades of difficulty. Routes in this region are often difficult to locate because of the lack of easily recognized prominent features. The most useful reference point is Deception Pillar located 200 or 300 yards left (south) of the Southeast Face.

At the left margin of the Southeast Face, a steep scree and rock gully ascends left about 100 or 200 feet to a saddle between the main face and a large detached buttress whose summit forms a small pinnacle about 15 feet above the saddle, and which bears the intriguing name Limp Dick (Route 15). Beyond the saddle to the southwest, the base of the rock slants downward for some distance. A large smooth face is found about 200 yards from the saddle. At its left edge is Deception Pillar (Route 8), a 200-foot buttress which is one of the largest rock structures in the southern complex.

On the left side of Deception Pillar is a prominent gully which provides one of the easier ways of descent in this region. At the top, a 20-foot step is negotiated by chimneying through a narrow hole into a cave below. Easy gully climbing follows until near the bottom. The lower 50 feet are very steep and are most easily descended by rappelling from a tree. Routes 3 to 7 are found on the left side of this gully above the rappel point. They are most easily approached by downclimbing the upper part of the gully. About 100 feet below the crawl hole in the gully, an 80-foot detached pillar (Le Dent) is seen on the southwest side. The routes are easily found with reference to this feature.

To the left of Deception Pillar, the well-broken South Face extends west for 200 or 300 yards. In two places it is broken by gullies or chutes which offer 3rd or 4th class routes to the summit. Between these is a little explored broken buttress which appears to offer some easy 5th class routes. At the westernmost end is a buttress which provides the most challenging routes of this group, Arpa Carpa and Wild Gazongas. To the left of this buttress easy scree leads to (or from) the top of the rock. Still farther west is a small isolated mass of rock with some good bouldering problems but no routes that merit listing. Below and slightly west of the Arpa Carpa buttress is a large rock with a few one or two-pitch routes on its south side. None of these is listed in the guide.

1. ARPA CARPA   Class 5.9

FA: May 1973; P. Warrender, J. Wilson, T. Sorenson, P. Cowan

This route is located on the westernmost buttress of Suicide Rock. Near the left edge of the buttress, a crack leads up some 50 feet. It is very thin at the start and the initial 20 feet are the most difficult. Above the crack, climb the face to a prominent belay ledge. It is possible to walk off left on easy rock to scree slopes, but Arpa Carpa continues by ascending a dihedral on the right to a bolt, followed by a difficult traverse right to a crack system leading to the top. In places protection is difficult and some medium angles may be advisable to supplement the usual chocks.

VARIATION

A short distance to the right of the first pitch, a separate crack system provides an equally difficult variation to the first pitch. First climbed by J. Long and R. Harrison.

2. WILD GAZONGAS   Class 5.10

FA: July 1973; R. Accomazzo, R. Harrison, J. Long

About 50 feet right of Arpa Carpa, two steep thin cracks mark the start of this route. Above these cracks continue up the face for 20 feet to a small ledge. Follow a thin crack to a difficult mantle, and traverse left and up 20 feet (5.10) to a bolt. Continue up and right past another bolt to a small belay ledge. Enjoyable 5.7 face climbing leads to the summit.

A number of stoppers between #2 and #7 will be needed, supplemented by a few thin horizontals and knifeblades.

3. MUNGE DIHEDRAL   Class 5.9

FA: T. Higgins, P. Ament

This route follows the obvious left-leaning jam crack immediately left of Le Dent.

4. FOREST LAWN   Class A2

FA: May 1973; P. Warrender, J. Wilson, T. Sorenson.

If you find the Munge Dihedral too grungy after the first few feet, you can follow an overhanging aid crack on the right. I was reluctant to classify this as a route, but have been assured that it is a fine exercise in aid climbing and therefore deserves recognition. Direct aid is difficult without using a few pitons—average horizontals up to 1½-inch angles.

5. ROOT CANAL   Class 5.7

FA: I. Couch, M. Dent

The left side of Le Dent consists of a long steep uniform enclosed chimney leading to a delightful belay spot above an overhang. Continue to the top of Le Dent and make a 5.6 move across to the main face.

6. LE DENT   Class 5.6

FA: I. Couch, J. Donini, M. Dent

Ascend the right side of the pillar of Le Dent. Easy chimneying leads to the top.

7. JAMMIT   Class 5.9

FA: J. Donini, I. Couch, M. Dent

Twenty feet right of Le Dent is a steep left facing dihedral
with an overhanging alcove at its base. This is Jammit.

8. DECEPTION PILLAR   Class 5.9

FA: July 1968; P. Callis, L. Harrell

Deception Pillar is the prominent 200-foot buttress described earlier which is found near the south margin of Suicide Rock. The climb begins by a large oak. The first pitch
ascends an obvious vertical crack system which splits the
buttress for about 70 feet. This part is deceptively difficult.
When the crack peters out continue up another 60 feet on
easier but less protected face climbing to a broad belay
ledge. The second pitch ascends an enjoyable chimney in
which several runners on horns can be used for protection.

   The quickest descent is by way of the gully on the left.
At the top, a 20-foot step is negotiated by chimneying
through a narrow hole into a cave below. A 50-foot rappel
from a tree delivers one to the starting point.

9. SHORT STORY   Class 5.6

FA: Unknown

A prominent dihedral is found between Deception Pillar and the smooth face on the right. Short Story follows the dihedral to the summit area of the rock. There is a difficult-looking section about halfway up. It can be surmounted by climbing a short slightly converging chimney on the right wall of the dihedral or by climbing even further right on difficult friction until a sharp rib can be followed back into the dihedral. The rest of the route is straightforward. A selection of about six nuts is adequate for the climb.

10. TWILIGHT DELIGHT   Class 5.9

FA: September 1974; C. Jacobs, T. Martin, D. Black

Between Short Story and Miscalculation there is a smooth face with two fine short routes. The first of these starts 50 to 100 feet right of Short Story in an obvious dihedral with a challenging four-inch lieback or jam crack. This leads to a broad ledge with a large dead tree. This point can also be reached by a 3rd or 4th class pitch just right of Short Story. From the east end of the ledge, climb diagonally up and left past two bolts to easier climbing and the last short pitch of Short Story. Slings around chockstones in the four-inch crack provide some protection, but you may wish to carry some extra large chocks to supplement these.

11. BOLTS TO NOWHERE   Class 5.11

FA: F. Ziel, N. Badyrka

This route is further right, ascending the very smooth face left of Miscalculation. The route is marked by bolts—further description is unnecessary. I have an unverified rumor that some or all of the bolts have been chopped, though I find this difficult to believe.

12. MISCALCULATION   Class 5.10+

FA: I. Couch, M. Dent

The smooth face to the right of Deception Pillar has several interesting dihedrals at its right margin. Miscalculation ascends the first of these left-facing dihedrals. The climbing is continuously difficult, little below 5.8 and somewhat difficult to protect. Small angles are useful.

13. SPRING CLEANING   Class 5.6

FA: I. Couch, M. Dent, L. Reynolds

Ascend the next dihedral right of Miscalculation. This crack initially contained hundreds of pounds of loose rock. It is now relatively clean and is a pleasant climb.

14. MAJOR   Class 5.7

FA: I. Couch, M. Dent

An interesting, low angle squeeze chimney is found 30 feet right of Spring Cleaning. A bolt protects the most difficult section at the top.

VARIATION—MINOR

An easy (class 5.1) low-angle crack is found just right of Major. Still farther right about 100 feet is a short easy 4th class gully. Since there is a tree at the top of the gully, it provides a convenient rappel route for descending. A single climbing rope doubled easily reaches the length of the gully.

JEFFREY PINE
Pinus jeffreyi

THE SMOOTH SOUL WALL

ROUTES 15–25

I do not know the source of the name for this portion of
Suicide Rock. It is detached from the rest of the rock by
broad tree-filled gullies on both sides. It appears prominently at the left margin of the photograph of Suicide Rock,
split by the deep Chatsworth Chimney (Route 20), and
topped by Limp Dick (Route 15). The wall on both sides of
the Chatsworth Chimney provides a number of short challenging face climbs.

15. LIMP DICK   Class 5.10

FA: May 1959; M. Powell, H. Daley, D. Rearick

This route leads to the summit of the large detached buttress to the left of the Southeast Face. Although the summit

is only about 15 feet above the saddle behind the buttress, this face is overhanging and does not appear to be climbable without aid. The outer face of the buttress is split by two large horizontal clefts about 100 feet below the summit which separate Limp Dick from the Smooth Soul Wall below. From the upper of these, ascend a short overhang with an awkward mantle to seemingly inadequate footholds. Traverse left and up following an obvious course to reach the open face and 100 feet of easy climbing though with little protection. At the top of the small overhang, an expansion bolt on the left provides the principal protection. Protection above is difficult without pitons (and even with them). The first free ascent of this route was made by T. Higgins in 1969.

VARIATION

Thirty feet right of the original route, an extended stem and strenuous mantle leads past a bolt to easier climbing. This 5.10 route was pioneered by J. Long in 1973.

16. LAST DANCE   Class 5.10

FA: E. Eriksson, W. Squires

At the bottom of the far left edge of the Smooth Soul Wall, a thin finger-jam leads directly up. Above face climbing leads to a fingertip lieback which is the crux of the climb. Small stoppers provide most of the protection but one or two knifeblades may be needed.

17. BLOWN OUT   Class 5.10+

FA: May 1972; G. Bender, P. Warrender

The next three routes all start from a prominent ledge found about 15 feet above the ground on the left part of the Smooth Soul Wall. This ledge runs nearly horizontally from the left and as it nears the Chatsworth Chimney it sweeps upward first to a small pillar or pedestal, and then up to the edge of the Chimney. Blown Out starts near the left end and proceeds up past four bolts, the hardest move being at the third bolt.

18. DOWN AND OUT   Class 5.10

FA: March 1974; G. Lewis, J. Wilson

From the top of the pillar or pedestal described in the previous route, diagonal left and up past two bolts. Continue more or less straight up past four more bolts to the top of the wall. As with the previous route, bolts provide all necessary protection.

19. DROWNED OUT   Class 5.9

FA: September 1972; J. Knutson, P. Warrender

From the starting pillar of Down and Out, continue up and right on the flake leading to the Chatsworth Chimney. Eventually climb left onto the face via a pothole. Climb up past three bolts, traverse right to the edge of Chatsworth Chimney and ascend this edge to the top.

20. CHATSWORTH CHIMNEY   Class 5.5

FA: Unknown

This chimney is the one referred to in the description of the Smooth Soul Wall. The major difficulty is found in the first 15 feet.

21. THE FIEND   Class 5.9

FA: June 1972; J. Wilson, P. Warrender

The face to the right of the Chatsworth Chimney is roughly speaking equally smooth everywhere, so that given protection, routes are possible almost arbitrarily. There are, however, five principal lines of bolts which define the next five routes. The Fiend starts a few feet right of the Chimney. Touching the Chimney is strictly off route. Ascending to the first bolt involves some tricky friction. From the bolt traverse right and then up past two more bolts. Continue up and left to the fourth bolt and then to the belay ledge of Mickey Mantle.

22. MICKEY MANTLE   Class 5.8

FA: April 1972; J. Wilson, P. Warrender

This delightful route starts in the middle of the Smooth Soul Wall, about 30 feet right of the Chatsworth Chimney. The route passes three bolts to a belay ledge. From the second bolt, traverse right until larger holds are found, then continue up and left. From the belay ledge a short easy pitch leads up and left through a chimney.

144

23. THE ULTIMATUM   Class 5.10

FA: April 1972; J. Long, G. Lewis

This route starts 50 feet right of the Chatsworth Chimney, just left of an ominous flake perched against the face. Moderate climbing leads up 20 feet to a bolt. A few difficult (5.9) moves lead to a knobby section and a second bolt. A series of improbable mantles lead 20 feet to a third bolt where more difficult climbing leads right and then up to a belay ledge. An easy ramp left leads to the top of the face. A long sling to lasso a huge knob will be useful.

24. PINK ROYD   Class 5.10+

FA: E. Eriksson, J. Long

Hopefully this is the last distinct route on the Smooth Soul Wall. Starting 35 feet right of Ultimatum, climb past a fixed pin and two bolts, the second bolt being the crux. This leads directly to Sensuous Corner which is followed to the top. One small to medium stopper can be used.

25. SENSUOUS CORNER   Class 5.9

FA: 1973; G. Lewis, G. Labadie

This route ascends the far right edge of the Smooth Soul Wall. Start at the large dead tree halfway up the right edge. Ascend a flared crack 30 feet and continue up interesting face climbing protected by a sling in an eye in the rock and a bolt. Several nuts small to medium.

THE SOUTHEAST
(SUNSHINE) FACE

ROUTES 26–42

This imposing face is easily identified by the large 60-foot block, Paisano Pinnacle, which caps its left side. This block is perched on the left end of a flat shelf, Paisano Ledge, which forms a break high on the face. A 20-foot sugar pine is found on this ledge, to the right of Paisano Pinnacle. Below Paisano ledge and located near the center of the face about 75 feet above the ground is another distinguishing landmark, Log Ledge, easily recognized without further description. The Southeast Face is bordered on the left by a gully whose condition on first ascent led to the quaint name Garbage Gulch (Route 26). On the right it is bordered by Buttress Chimney (Route 42). Between these are a number of face routes which are the most spectacular on the rock and which provide exceptionally fine face climbing challenges. Most of the routes end at Paisano Ledge. From this ledge a few routes lead to the summit of the rock; the one most commonly used is Continuation (Route 64).

Descent from the summit area above the Southeast Face can be made quickly by a 150-foot rappel from a Jeffrey pine near the top of Continuation down to Paisano Ledge. Descent from the ledge is easily accomplished by down-climbing Bye Gully (Route 61). Many climbers will not feel a rope necessary for the very short class 5 pitch on this route.

26. GARBAGE GULCH   Class 5.1

FA: G. Harr and others

Immediately left of Paisano Chimney (Route 31) is a broad easy gully, narrowing at the top.

27. THE SOURCE   Class 5.10

FA: I. Couch, M. Dent

A left-leaning flared shallow slot is found 50 feet left and above the Ouch Chimney. The chief difficulties are face climbing into the slot (5.10), and awkward jamming to exit (5.9).

28. CHISHOLM TRAIL   Class 5.11

FA: 1957; F. Ziel, T. Powell

The Chisholm Trail is a difficult face climb between the Source and the Ouch Chimney. Climb over a bulge to a flake crack. Lieback up 40 or 50 feet to reach a bolt which protects the climbing above.

29. BC'S OUCH CHIMNEY   Class 5.9

FA: I. Couch, M. Cohen, R. Kamps

Near the bottom of Garbage Gulch, and left of Paisano Chimney, is a long vertical shallow wide-flaring chimney with a fin of rock at its right edge. The most difficult section is a short overhanging section one-third of the way up.

30. THE MAN WHO FELL TO EARTH   Class 5.10+

FA: 1978; E. Eriksson, T. Powell

This is another difficult face climb just right of BC's Ouch Chimney. From the top of a flake or tall pedestal, climb through an area of thin cracks to an open face. Three bolts protect the difficult 5.10 climbing above.

31. PAISANO CHIMNEY   Class 5.8

FA: May 1968; P. Callis, L. Harrell

At the left border of the Southeast Face, a 150-foot crack and chimney system leads directly to the left side of Paisano Pinnacle. The main technical difficulty is the starting overhang. About 20 feet up care should be used in passing a loose block. From the top of the chimney, climb behind Paisano Pinnacle to Paisano Ledge.

32. EUPHORIA   Class 5.6 & A2

FA: I. Couch, M. Dent

Between Paisano Chimney and the Drain Pipe is a massive
flake system leading up one or two pitches to the base of
Paisano Pinnacle about 50 feet left of the Paisano Overhang
(Route 44). To surmount the overhang of Paisano Pinnacle,
two bolts and one piton for aid can be used. Above the overhang, easy but spectacular face climbing leads to the top of
Paisano Pinnacle.

33. GATES OF DELIRIUM   Class 5.11

FA: January 1976; T. Yaniro, D. Leversee

The lower part of this route follows a nearly direct line between Paisano Chimney and the Drain Pipe. From a point
some 30 feet left of the Drain Pipe variation, climb directly
up past two bolts to a small dihedral protected by fixed pitons. Continue diagonally right to the beginning ledge of
the Drain Pipe. Face climbing above gains entrance to a fun
crack protected by a bolt and a few fixed pins. At the top of
the crack, traverse right past a bolt to a good belay ledge.
Either of two cracks is then followed to the base of Paisano
Pinnacle. The final traverse right to Paisano Ledge is an interesting ending for a splendid route. A wide range of
chocks should be carried, and possibly a few pitons in case
the fixed pin placement is too sparse.

34. THE DRAIN PIPE   Class 5.7 & A1 or 5.11

FA: March 1967; L. Harrell, C. Raymond

This route ascends the soaring crack which leads up to the center of the overhang formed by the base of Paisano Pinnacle. The route starts from a narrow ledge 50 feet above the base of the Southeast Face. This ledge is easily identified by a 20-foot sugar pine growing on it. To reach the ledge, climb down from the recess at the base of Paisano Chimney. From the right end, early ascents used a hook and a piton in an incipient crack to reach an S-shaped crack which is ascended easily by direct aid to a point where moderate face climbing leads right to a ledge at the base of the main crack. With deterioration of the small incipient crack, a bolt was placed to give easier access to the S-shaped crack. It is possible to ascend this face free, though it is very difficult 5.11 climbing. The first free ascent was made by J. Long and R. Harrison in 1973.

The exhilarating pitch up the drainpipe is easier than it looks. At the top, traverse right under the Paisano overhang.

VARIATION   Class A3

A short direct aid pitch can be used as a variation to reach the beginning ledge. Start at the large oak tree 75 feet below and slightly right of this ledge. A difficult mantle to a small ledge is followed by four aid bolts which give access to a thin 30-foot crack. Piton placement in the crack is reported to be quite difficult. From the top of the crack, an easy traverse brings one to the regular route.

35. QUIET DESPERATION   Class 5.11

FA: March 1976; G. Lewis, R. Accomazzo, J. Wilson

The smooth Southeast Face between the Drainpipe and the

right edge contains about a half dozen of the finest face climbs on Suicide Rock, all rated between 5.10 and 5.11 in difficulty. The first two start with the same first pitch. From the start of the Drainpipe Variation, walk right 50 feet on a broad ledge. Chimney to the top of a spectacular flake and ascend a very difficult left leaning crack to gain a ledge some 40 feet above. This point is about 50 feet above and left of Log Ledge.

An incredibly thin flake diagonals up and left. Initial protection is via the first bolt on the Iron Cross to the right. Continue along the flake past another bolt to open face climbing protected by three more bolts. The last pitch is a beautiful lieback ending at Paisano Ledge.

36. THE IRON CROSS   Class 5.10+

FA: May 1968; C. Raymond, P. Callis

This route follows a nearly vertical line, ending just a few feet right of Paisano Pinnacle. Start as in the previous route, walking right about 50 feet on a broad ledge from a point near the Drainpipe Variation. Chimney to the top of a spectacular flake and ascend a very difficult left leaning crack to a ledge some 40 feet above.

From the right end of the ledge climb a tricky difficult-to-protect dihedral. A series of four bolts protects the climbing on the blank face above. Passing the second bolt is one of the crux moves—the name of the route is derived from the body position usually assumed to execute it. A delicate traverse left from the fourth bolt is even more difficult, and is often done with aid. The traverse leads to a slanting dihedral which provides 30 feet of easier climbing. Above are four more bolts which protect the difficult face climbing

to Paisano Ledge. The first free ascent of this route was
made in 1973.

37. SUNDANCE   Class 5.10

FA: January 1967; P. Callis, C. Raymond, L. Harrell

Sundance ascends the Southeast Face from its base to the
right end of Paisano Ledge via Log Ledge and a short crescent shaped dihedral at midface. It parallels the Iron Cross
which is about 50 feet to the left. On the first pitch ascend
an inside corner and traverse up and right 20 feet to the left
corner of Log Ledge which is gained by a short but strenuous 5.8 lieback. From the left edge of Log Ledge make a
difficult move up past a bolt. Easier climbing leads 15 feet to
another bolt. Traverse right to a chicken head and follow
past three bolts until even with the lower end of the dihedral. A 5.9 traverse 15 feet to the right ends at the crescent
dihedral. Climb part way up, exiting to the right as soon as
possible. Easier climbing leads to a pair of belay bolts. The
third pitch continues 40 feet past two bolts and then follows
a crack to Paisano Ledge.

38. VALHALLA   Class 5.11

FA: November 1970; I. Couch, L. Reynolds, M. Dent

Valhalla starts at a pine tree on a ledge below the right hand
end of Log Ledge. This point is about 30 feet to the left of
First Pitch (See New Generation). A difficult mantle leads to
steep face climbing past two bolts. A sloping ledge leads up
and right to a third bolt. From here climb left and up to Log
Ledge, the end of the first pitch. Move out right on a hori-

zontal crack 15 feet to a bolt on the blank face. The crux of the climb is found in the next 20 feet of difficult face moves. Difficult face climbing with bolt protection continues for 70 feet to a two-bolt hanging belay.

Traverse left to the lower end of the dihedral of Sundance, and then climb up 25 feet staying about ten feet right of Sundance. Traverse back right to another bolt and continue up. Here additional protection can be obtained by climbing over to a Sundance bolt and traversing back. One more bolt leads to the entrance into "Valhalla" and easier climbing to Paisano Ledge. This remarkable face climb combines technical difficulty with great natural beauty. It was probably the first 5.11 route at Suicide Rock.

39. NEW GENERATION   Class 5.11

FA: July 1973; M. Graham, T. Sorenson

About 30 feet right and below Log Ledge is another prominent ledge formerly called "No Go Ledge." Earlier editions of the guide described The First Pitch, a short class 5.7 jam crack leading from the lowest point on the face to the left end of No Go Ledge. For seven years no progress was made beyond this point. Now another fine 5.11 route parallels and rivals Valhalla and other variations between Valhalla and Hesitation appear possible. The first climbers of the New Generation did not even take advantage of the easy 5.7 jam crack at the left edge of No Go Ledge, but chose to ascend the difficult face about 20 feet to the right. Climbing past the three bolts to No Go Ledge may be difficult 5.10, but it is only a warm-up for what follows. The crux of the climb is in the first 40 feet of the next pitch. From the center of the ledge, climb straight up past three bolts ending the pitch at the belay stance and bolt of Hesitation. The third pitch passes four bolts in a slightly zigzag pattern, crossing the Stretch just below the top.

40. HESITATION   Class 5.10

FA: July 1967; P. Callis

Hesitation ascends the far right side of the Southeast Face. The normal route begins by traversing up and left out of Buttress Chimney along a prominent ramp or trough which starts about 80 feet above the ground. At the end of this zone of weakness, traverse left a few feet and climb up 15 feet on large holds to a belay point (bolt anchor). The next pitch leads diagonally up and left for about 40 feet, and then diagonally up and right approximately 60 feet to a left curving crack and ledge system. Four bolts and two runners on chicken heads give good protection on this challenging pitch. As the name suggests, a move between the third and fourth bolt will probably cause you to pause for at least a short moment. The last pitch follows cracks and ledges coincident with the Stretch to Paisano Ledge.

VARIATION—HESITATION DIRECT   Class 5.10 +

Another exit from No Go Ledge ascends from the right end of the ledge past four bolts to the first belay on the regular route. This difficult beginning was first climbed by J. Long and E. Errikson in 1975.

VARIATION—VOODOO CHILD   Class 5.11

Use the same exit from No Go Ledge as Hesitation Direct. At or just below the second bolt, a very difficult diagonal traverse up and left leads to a single bolt in the middle of the face. Unprotected 5.8 climbing leads directly up to Paisano Ledge.

41. THE STRETCH   Class 5.9

FA: November 1966; P. Callis, C. Raymond, P. Raymond

From the notch behind the East Buttress, descend a few feet into Buttress Chimney and climb out to the left ascending an easy 75-foot crack to the left end of a ledge next to the fir tree in Bye Gully (Route 61). The second pitch ascends the airy crest of the Southeast Face on large holds for 30 to 40 feet using one runner for protection. A bolt protects an extended move left into a left-curving crack which is then followed to Paisano Ledge.

42. BUTTRESS CHIMNEY   Class 5.6

FA: Unknown

This route ascends the deep chimney between the Southeast Face and the East Buttress ending at the Notch behind the East Buttress. The first few feet are tricky (5.6). The easy chimney above is blocked by a giant chockstone which is, however, easily passed on the right (class 5.5).

THE PAISANO PINNACLE

ROUTES 43–47

Paisano Pinnacle is the 60-foot block perched on the left end of Paisano Ledge at the top of the Southeast Face. Part of its base overhangs the face below, forming a spectacular roof and one of the more challenging routes at Suicide. Five routes have been used to reach its summit. Euphoria (Route 32) starts near the base of the Southeast Face and has been described earlier in the guide. Three of the others are simply routes up the pinnacle starting from Paisano Ledge and may be combined with any other route leading to this point. The easiest approach is Bye Gully (Route 61). Descent of the pinnacle is best made by downclimbing a short distance along the northeast edge and rappelling from a bolt.

43. STEP AWAY   Class 5.7

FA: November 1966; C. Raymond, P. Callis

Paisano Pinnacle is separated from the main face by a narrow slot which is the ideal width for chimney climbing. From a point in the slot near the northwest corner of the pinnacle, chimney diagonally south and up until some protection can be placed high in a crack near the southwest corner of the pinnacle. At this point one may either climb the crack or make a more exposed but easier step across at the corner to easy scrambling.

44. PAISANO OVERHANG   Class A3 or 5.12

FA: January 1968; P. Callis, C. Raymond

The three- or four-inch crack which forms the Paisano Jam Crack extends entirely through the pinnacle, providing another route on the exhilarating, exposed East Face. Early ascents were made using three- to four-inch bongs for aid under the ten-foot roof and for the first ten feet on the east face of the pinnacle. Above 5.7 climbing leads to the summit.

The first free ascent by J. Long in 1973 has rarely, if ever, been repeated by other climbers. Two four-inch bongs were driven for protection, their placement being almost as challenging as the climb itself.

45. PAISANO JAM CRACK   Class 5.9

FA: February 1955; M. Powell, D. Wilson, F. Hoover

Paisano Pinnacle is cleaved by a remarkably uniform three- to four-inch crack which passes through the entire block a few feet from its north side. The 20-foot jam crack on the inside face was reported to be class 5.8 by the first ascent party. They, however, had three advantages—a snowbank (which shortened the difficult section and cushioned their falls), mountain boots (which fit well into the crack), and a jug of paisano (to keep up their spirits). The latter was left on the summit devoid of its contents. Sober climbers in kletterschuhe have found the crack to be considerably more difficult. A couple of three- or four-inch bongs or chocks are necessary to protect the crack in the absence of a snowbank. After the jam crack, scramble up 40 feet to the summit. A few remnants of the jug can still be found on the summit.

46. MANTLE OF NO RETURN   Class 5.8 to 5.9

FA: October 1973; J. Wilson, G. Lewis, K. Cooper

From the rappel hooks on the wall behind Paisano Pinnacle, descend until it is possible to lean across, hopefully reaching a small bowl. The difficulty of the mantle varies inversely with the height of the climber. Somewhere below five feet, six inches it may even become impossible.

47. SUPERFLY   Class 5.8?

First crossing: W. Antel, M. Graham, T. Sorenson,
     R. Accomazzo.

A climbing route? Maybe not, but it is an outrageously elegant way to get off of Paisano Pinnacle. From the top of the pinnacle make a running leap to the opposite wall, and climb to the top. If the climber succeeds in lassoing the rappel hooks high on the wall before the leap, the protection is somewhat improved.

THE EAST BUTTRESS
(BUTTRESS OF CRACKS)

ROUTES 48–60

The lowest point on Suicide Rock is the base of a steep buttress which extends approximately halfway (150 feet) up
the right-hand border of the Southeast Face. A shallow
notch separates the summit of the buttress from the rock
behind at the juncture of the Southeast and East Faces. The
Notch and the summit of the buttress can be reached trival-
ly from the base of the East Face.

Most of the routes on this buttress lie along closely
spaced parallel cracks. Because of this and the lack of distinguishing landmarks at the base of each climb, the begin-
nings of routes are not generally described independently.
The climber may find it simplest to locate all of the routes
by identifying them in sequence starting with Insomnia.

48. INSOMNIA   Class 5.11

FA: June 1967; P. Callis, L. Reynolds

This remarkable uniform crack breaks the otherwise flaw-less southwest face of the East Buttress. Its first ascent caused the loss of at least 300 bat-hours of sleep. The route begins in an overhanging dihedral which is reached by traversing right from a point 30 feet up the Buttress Chimney (Route 42). The first 25 feet is moderate 5.8 free climbing. Above, the route is sometimes climbed using many pitons and nuts for direct aid (class A3). The first free ascent was made by J. Erickson in 1972, using only nuts for protection. Most expert climbers have been able to repeat this feat. For a person with the required physical strength, it is easier than it looks, but it still ranks in the 5.11 range.

49. DOUBLE EXPOSURE   Class 5.11

FA: T. Sorenson, G. Lewis, K. Casper

The route on the sharp corner between the southwest and southeast faces of the East Buttress is called Double Exposure. The original ascent started at the bottom of Insomnia, traversed across the southeast face using two bolts for aid, and after three bolts on the 5.10 corner, joined the Pirate near the top. The entire length of the corner can be climbed, although the upper and lower sections are considerably more difficult. The upper section was first climbed by J. Long in 1975. One bolt was added 60 feet above the original bolts, and intermediate protection was obtained by traversing over to the Pirate to place some chocks. The lower section now rated 5.11 was first climbed by T. Yaniro in 1978. Some protection below the first bolt can be achieved by throwing a sling over a horn.

50. THE PIRATE   Class 5.8 & A2 or 5.12

FA: November 1966; P. Callis, L. Reynolds

Ten feet right of the sharp corner between the southwest and southeast faces of the East Buttress, a beautiful thin 100-foot crack bisects an otherwise perfectly blank section of rock. As originally climbed, about 20 direct aid pitons were used to reach the level of a ledge under a roof on the right. The popularity of the climb and the usual overdriving of alloy steel pitons has resulted in a crack so pockmarked with piton holes that it can be climbed now using nuts only. Even more remarkable, T. Yaniro in 1978 was able to lead the entire pitch free, although there was extreme difficulty of chock placement because of lack of places to pause or stop. If climbed without protection in place, the route probably deserves a rating of 5.12.

At the top of the first pitch, make a long step right to a ledge and belay from a bolt. To continue, cross back to the crack and continue 15 feet to the left where small holds offer interesting 5.8 climbing for 15 or 20 feet. To protect this exposed lead, place a good chock or pin as high as possible when crossing the crack. Above, an interesting crack continues to the top.

51. CAPTAIN HOOK   Class 5.7

FA: October 1966; C. Raymond, L. Reynolds

Captain Hook follows the chimney 20 feet right of the Pirate. The first lead is finished by passing an overhang (the Crocodile's Head) to an alcove. Above, ascend the slippery chimney (the Throat) to the summit of the buttress.

52. PASS TIME   Class 5.9

FA: March 1968; P. Gleason, L. Harrell

From a point about eight feet up Captain Hook step right three feet into an adjacent crack. Eighty feet of interesting and sometimes tricky climbing in this crack leads to a ledge at the base of the Throat on Captain Hook. Continue up this route to the summit of the buttress.

53. FRUSTRATION   Class 5.10

FA: March 1968; P. Callis, L. Harrell

Fifteen feet to the right of the chimney of Captain Hook, there are two closely adjacent cracks which diverge upward. Frustration follows the right hand crack except at the very bottom where both cracks are used. The first 15 feet are particularly strenuous, especially if adequate protection is to be placed without resorting to direct aid. Above, the climbing continues to be difficult until a belay ledge is reached 60 feet above the ground. The chimney and crack above lead to a ledge from which one may continue to the top on Captain Hook or East Buttress Gully.

54. THE SWORD OF DAMOCLES   Class 5.8 or 5.9

FA: March 1968; J. Gosling, L. Harrell

Fifteen feet right of Frustration is another crack system. Climb up ten feet, traverse right eight feet and ascend to a prominent crack which leads up to an obvious slot about 50 feet off the ground. The left-hand edge of the slot is a large sword-like flake completely detached and resting on a small pedestal. The need to avoid this flake makes this point the crux of the climb. From a ledge 20 feet above the sword, lie-back up a very thin flake to another ledge. Continue to the top via East Buttress Gully.

55. HERNIA   Class 5.8

FA: August 1967; L. Harrell, S. Wood

Hernia follows the northernmost crack system on the southeast face of the buttress and lies generally about 20 feet right of the Sword of Damocles. It starts just left of the lowest point on Suicide Rock. Ascend broken rock 40 feet and follow the crack which continues up about 60 feet and passes out of sight around the corner to the right. Following an interesting traverse join the East Buttress Gully near the beginning of Route 56. This climb can be completed in one pitch (barely) if a 150-foot rope is used.

Three variations have been reported on this route: two at the start and one at the end. The first starts about 20 feet right of the Hernia crack and leads up and then left to the crack. One bolt and one piton protect this class 5.8 pitch (J. Hoagland, D. Bird). The second variation, called ARSY FARCY, also starts on the right. The three bolts make this 5.10 route obvious (M. Kaeser, G. Bender, P. Warrender, J. Wilson).

The third variation takes off near the top where the regular route traverses right to Buttress Gully. A bolt protects a difficult 5.9 move straight up which leads to easy beautiful face climbing (I. Couch, M. Dent).

165

56. EAST BUTTRESS GULLY   Class 5.2

FA: Unknown

A prominent chute or gully leads up the northeast side of the East Buttress. Halfway up pass two large trees (a sugar pine and a cedar) growing close together in the bottom of the chute. Above several variations are possible. Two or three chocks may be used for protection.

57. THE PLAGUE   Class 5.7

FA: July 1971; F. Ziel, N. Humphrey, C. Pedigo

There are a number of possibilities for an enjoyable two-pitch climb on the narrow face just right of East Buttress Gully. The first route reported here started from the lowest point of the face and proceeded up and left using several bolts for protection. Since the first ascent, other climbers have chopped out all of the bolts. Although it may be true that the number of bolts was excessive by their standards, the other extreme of removing all the bolts is a far greater crime. The lead is about 5.6 in difficulty and extends up the face perhaps 30 or 40 feet before any protection is possible. Many climbers will be intimidated from attempting this interesting moderate route without at least some protection.

    Start near the lowest point of the face and climb up and left to a crack. Ascend the crack to its end and cross left to a small tree. Climb the crack above until it is possible to move right on good holds to a wide belay ledge. It has been pointed out that the now unprotected first lead can be eliminated by starting up a narrow jam crack on the left about 20 or 30 feet up Buttress Gully. A much more interesting alternative is the obvious left-facing dihedral at the right margin of the face. This crack can be ascended (class 5.6) by lieback, jamming and chimneying to the top of the dihedral. Ascend the short ten-foot face directly above on small holds to reach the prominent belay ledge described in the first route. A third alternative is to ascend the face just left of the dihedral. Although it appears at first glance to be blank, the climbing probably does not exceed 5.3 or 5.4 in difficulty except for the ten-foot face at the top mentioned above. One can also stay in the middle of the face between these variations. One bolt should be in place about 45 feet from the ground. The climbing is about 5.9 in difficulty above the bolt.

For the second pitch traverse left along the ledge to a tight slightly overhanging chimney. The initial move looks difficult, but the climbing rapidly eases, with face climbing leading to a second belay ledge. Third class scrambling leads to the summit of East Buttress.

58. ZUCCHINIS FROM ALPHA CENTAURI

Class 5.10

FA: July 1975; J. Wilson, P. Wilkening, R. Shockley

The large belay ledge of the Plague extends to the right to join the talus slope below the Weeping Wall. Two short difficult one-pitch routes are found at this corner. Zucchinis is just left of the corner. Ascend a steep face to a flake with a bolt at its top. Traverse left and up to reach easy scrambling.

59. LOW PRESSURE   Class 5.10

FA: T. Sorenson, G. Lewis

Low Pressure is found just right of the corner described above. Ascend an interesting dihedral by 5.10 lieback, undercling the roof to the right and continue up a 5.8 jam-crack to easy scrambling.

60. WARM UP   Class 5.8

FA: August 1970; R. Lindgren, E. Evans, R. DeRusha

A prominent vertical crack on the north face of the East Buttress begins five feet above the ground, just east of the bottom of Bye Gully, and ends about 30 feet above at a large ledge. Easy scrambling leads to the top of the Buttress. This was originally protected with angle pitons. I am not sure how well it can be protected with chocks.

THE EAST FACE
(THE WEEPING WALL)

ROUTES 61–77

This magnificent 300-foot slab of light colored water-streaked rock offers some exceptionally fine friction climbing. The spectacular flared chimney and its associated cracks at the right of the face also present some intriguing challenges. An important landmark is a small oak tree at the base of the face on its right side. Samson, Goliath and David (Routes 71 to 73) start at this tree. To descend one can make a 150-foot rappel from a tree just to the north of the ledge at the top of Goliath and David. This places the climber on the chute or tree-covered ledge of the Escalator which can be easily climbed down to the base of the rock.

61. BYE GULLY   **Class 5.5**

FA: Unknown

Bye Gully forms the left border of the East Face, and lies

just right of the Southeast Face. The route leads from the Notch behind the East Buttress to Paisano Ledge. The climb is easy class 3 scrambling except for a 10-foot flared chimney halfway up. The inexperienced may find this section quite challenging to climb up, but it may be descended much more easily. It is routinely climbed down by experienced climbers without belay.

62. MUSHY PEACH   Class 5.10

FA: 1978; R. Leavitt, P. Neal

Three routes have been used to reach the top of the rock from Paisano Ledge. They are closely spaced and are located just right of Paisano Pinnacle. Mushy Peach is the leftmost route. It is a very nice face climb protected by three bolts.

63. SKIGLIACK   Class 5.9

FA: July 1971; D. Hanbury, D. Black

At the right end of Paisano Ledge, broken rock leads up the face. This is the starting point for both Skigliack and Continuation. Skigliack ascends up and left along a small white ramp to its end. After an extended move left climb up past two bolts to the bucket just beneath the bolt on Continuation. Continue left and up along a shallow groove which runs parallel to and ten feet left of the Continuation.

64. CONTINUATION   Class 5.6

FA: Unknown

This enjoyable one-pitch route leads up the broken slabs from Paisano Ledge to the summit of Suicide Rock. Start on the right north end of the ledge. After 50 feet of climbing a bolt protects an interesting friction move up to a shallow groove leading to the summit.

65. COMMENCEMENT   Class 5.9

FA: May 1970; R. Kamps, I. Couch

Just right of Bye Gully (Route 61), a 150-foot slab lies against the Weeping Wall. The top of this slab is reached by easy climbing on its face. Drop down on the right edge about six feet and follow a crack up and right about 20 feet to a small ledge below a right arching flake. A piton under this arch protects difficult (5.9) face climbing up and left 30 feet to a ledge. Continue directly up on easier climbing to the bolt on Continuation and follow this route to the top.

66. CLAM CHOWDER   Class 5.8

FA: May 1973; J. Smith, B. Foster, J. Wood, C. Jacobs

Starting from the left, this is the first of five or six routes that ascend the main face of the Weeping Wall. A good starting point is about 15 feet from the left edge where a three-foot incipient crack is found. Climb 70 feet to a ledge and expansion bolt. (This bolt is often used by climbers ascending Surprise, though it is to the left of that route and was not used on the early ascents). Ascend 50 feet to another bolt. Traverse left a few feet to a rib. Climb up and left to a hole and another bolt. Continue up past three bolts then traverse right to some solution pockets leading to a small ledge. Climb straight up an incipient crack (one bolt) to a tree which marks the end of the route. Protection is provided entirely by bolts.

67. SURPRISE   Class 5.8

FA: April 1966; P. Callis, L. Reynolds

Surprise is believed to be the first major face route on Suicide Rock. It is an excellent introduction to Suicide Rock for the intermediate climber visiting for the first time. As one proceeds up the improbable looking route, each difficulty yields to some well-hidden secret. The difficult parts of the route are protected by chocks or fixed pins except at one point where a bolt protects the most difficult move.

The route begins near a small fir tree at the center of the base of the East Face. Climb up 15 feet on large holds left of a crack. A chock or piton may be placed high in this crack to protect an interesting friction move up and left. Above, climbing becomes easier, but protection is lacking for the next 70 feet. Here a ledge is reached where short thick pitons were formerly used to anchor a belay. It is now simpler to traverse left a few feet and use the belay bolt of Clam Chowder. Traverse to the right end of the ledge and climb 20 feet up to a bolt which protects a series of interesting friction moves on a ridge of crystals (class 5.8). Easier climbing leads up 25 feet to a lieback crack. From the top of the crack traverse left and belay at the base of a prominent trough. The third pitch ascends this trough on good holds to the summit of the rock.

VARIATION   Class 5.9

Instead of traversing left near the end of the second pitch of Surprise, traverse right to a pronounced rib and belay from a pair of bolts. A long lead past three bolts ends at a belay position where another bolt will be found about 30 feet below the summit. This variation was first climbed by P. Callis and M. Dent in 1966.

68. REVELATION   Class 5.9

FA: August 1970; I. Couch, M. Dent

Two of the most popular routes on the Weeping Wall are Revelation and Serpentine located just right of Surprise. Unlike the latter, these routes are as blank as they look. Each involves nearly 300 feet of continuous challenging face climbing as it winds its way past a procession of about 15 or 16 bolts. Although both are now rated 5.9, Revelation on the left is distinctly more difficult.

Revelation begins at the base of the thin crack at the start of Surprise. Climb the face just right of this crack using it for protection. From its top, climb directly up, but avoid bearing left to the easy rock of Surprise. Three bolts protect this section, the second bolt of this route being the third bolt of Serpentine. Two bolts for a belay are found below an obvious thin, dark dihedral. Climb the dihedral using additional bolts for protection. While no individual move on the second pitch is harder than 5.9, there are many moves of 5.8 and 5.9 difficulty. The second and third pitches ascend directly up the face, always staying between the Surprise Variation and Serpentine. The hardest single move is found on the third pitch.

VARIATION   Class 5.10

A more difficult variation of this route is due to M. Woerner. Directly above the starting point of Surprise and Revelation, one of the watermarks streaking the rock is seen to have a distinct orange tint. Woerner's route takes a direct line up the orange streak with no deviations except an occasional move on the white flakey area to the right about halfway up. The three pitches are protected by bolts which are independent of the two adjacent routes.

69. SERPENTINE   Class 5.9

FA: 1967; P. Callis, L. Harrell

Serpentine snakes its way up the East Face to the right of Revelation. Climbing begins near the right edge of the face by an oak tree. From the first bolt 20 feet above, climb diagonally up and left past a second bolt to the third bolt. This bolt is also used on Revelation which continues more or less directly up from this point. Serpentine swings back right and continues up as indicated by the line of bolts. The hardest move is just above the seventh bolt. The fifth and twelfth bolts are doubled for belaying.

70. TEN KARAT GOLD   Class 5.10

FA: June 1973; J. Long, R. Harrison, R. Accomazzo,
   D. Watson

There really isn't room for another route between Serpentine and Sampson, but this is too fine a climb to reject.
Twenty-five feet above Litter Ledge is a small prominent
ledge extending left from the Sampson dihedral. From the
left end follow a prominent gold streak past two bolts. Diagonal right to a third bolt and then straight up an obvious
weakness for 50 or 60 feet. Traverse right 25 feet to a small
ledge where a fixed piton protects the move up to the "win-
dow pane," the smoothest most featureless section of the
Weeping Wall. Continuous 5.9 edging and friction lead to
the last bolt. The route has seven or eight bolts in place, two
thin pitons (hopefully fixed). It is two or three pitches long
depending on the rope length.

71. SAMPSON   Class 5.9

FA: August 1967; P. Callis, L. Harrell

Sampson follows the obvious dihedral forming the right
margin of the blank East Face. It lies just left of the prominent flaring chimney of Goliath. The first pitch begins a few
feet right of the Serpentine. Several difficult moves on wa-
ter-polished rock lead straight up above the oak tree to an
easy trough which ends on a ledge system common to David
and Goliath. The second pitch ascends a smooth groove for
another 100 feet to a comfortable ledge at the base of the
main dihedral. The third pitch is the crux. The right wall of

the dihedral is smooth and vertical, the slab is polished, protection is difficult to place. Climbing is unrelenting 5.7 for over 100 feet until the right wall curves around to the left forcing the climber to make a strenuous mantle to reach the final belay ledge. It is difficult to protect this part without using direct aid.

72. GOLIATH   Class 5.7

FA: June 1966; C. Raymond, P. Callis

Goliath ascends the giant flaring chimney just beyond the right border of the East Face. Starting from the oak tree ascend an easy grassy groove diagonally to the right to a good belay ledge. A tricky move gives access to a 50-foot narrow chimney leading to the base of the main chimney. One may protect this final pitch well by staying back in the narrow part of the chimney but one pays for this security by considerable physical exertion. By staying out in the wide part, one may climb with relative ease.

73. DAVID   Class 5.7

FA: June 1966; C. Raymond, P. Callis

The route of David follows the smaller crack which runs parallel to and just right of Goliath. The first pitch is the same as for Goliath. The crux for this route is to surmount the overhanging lip of the dihedral of Goliath in order to gain access to the base of the crack of David above. It is surprisingly easy if one is aggressive about it. The climbing above is superb. One can climb on the crack or on the face immediately to the right. There are several good belay spots in the crack, and if one extends the second lead, the summit may be reached on the third pitch.

VARIATION—MOGEN DAVID   Class 5.8

Start 20 feet right of the normal beginning of David and Goliath. Thin cracks lead first to a black ledge and then up to the main crack of David. Thin stoppers are needed to protect the upper part of the pitch.

74. REBOLTING DEVELOPMENT   Class 5.10+

FA: October 1971; D. Wert, M. Kaeser, G. Bander

This fine friction route is found on the narrow face between David and Delila. The route involves interesting friction and edging past 12 bolts. No pitons are necessary. It is reported that the first bolt is now rather high up on the rock and that until another bolt is placed, the most dangerous part of the ascent is simply getting started.

75. DELILA   Class 5.8

FA: January 1968, P. Callis, C. Raymond, P. Raymond

About 50 feet right of the large left-facing dihedral containing Sampson is a difficult-looking, right-facing open book which forms this route. Several feet of interesting climbing in a steep trough lead to a platform. From this point the low angle chute of the Escalator leads diagonally to the right. Instead of following this chute, ascend the open book directly above. A difficult move near the bottom is followed by an easier but tiring lieback. After completing the lieback, climb up and slightly left to a good belay ledge. A second and final pitch ascends a second open book and easy slabs to a broad ledge.

76. SEASON'S END   Class 5.11

FA: T. Sorenson, M. Graham

Another fine face climb is found on the face to the right of Delilah. Ascend the first 20 feet of the Escalator and Delilah. A series of five bolts leads up the smooth face. On the first ascent, a diagonal traverse left to easier climbing was made at the fifth bolt. This gives a shorter route of 5.10 difficulty. In 1978, E. Eriksson was able to continue straight up using additional bolts for protection. This part of the route is reported to be 5.11 in difficulty.

77. DILEMMA   Class A3

FA: J. Long, J. Wilson

This difficult aid route is found on the left side of the Escalator chimney. Just beyond the halfway point in the chimney, a prominent white watercourse is found on the nearly vertical face, emerging from a long thin crack which ends 20 feet above the floor of the chimney. Interesting hooking leads to the crack which is followed 40 feet to a belay stance. Traverse right ten feet along another thin crack to a prominent trough. Easy climbing follows. A number of pitons or special aid hardware appear mandatory on this route.

178

THE NORTHERN AREA
ESCALATOR GROUP

ROUTES 78–90

The northernmost part of Suicide Rock has a wide variety of climbing terrain. The shorter routes of this area offer an interesting afternoon diversion when descending from the summit after one of the major routes. The main landmarks are the tree-covered ledge on the Escalator (Route 78), Eagle Pinnacle near the center, and Cat's Cave Inn (Route 103) an impressive right-facing dihedral at the north edge of the rock. About a dozen routes start from the base of the rock and end on the Escalator.

78. THE ESCALATOR   Class 5.6

FA: Unknown

This route coincides with Delila for the first 20 feet. Several feet of interesting climbing in a steep trough lead to a platform. The trough on the left is considerably easier. However, in winter and spring it is usually wet and one must climb the trough on the right which involves a 5.7 move. Beyond this the climbing is very easy. Ascend the narrow low angle chute diagonally up and right from the platform. Continue up and right a few hundred feet across easy tree-covered ledges. From a number of points on these ledges the summit may be attained by a short pitch of slightly harder climbing. This route serves mainly as a descent route. It is often descended unroped, but many climbers will want a belay over the bottom 15 feet.

79. JACKAL   Class 5.9

FA: November 1971; M. Kaeser, P. Warrender, J. Lonnie, T. Emerson

The Jackal starts in the shallow water chute a few feet right of the Escalator. An unusual lieback leads up to a prominent crack which continues up and right. From the end of this crack continue up another crack to the top of the climb on the Escalator ledge.

80. THE BREEZE   Class 5.8

FA: February 1968; C. Raymond, P. Raymond, J. Taylor

Fifty feet to the right of the base of the Escalator a break in the smooth face can be climbed to the base of a shallow chimney approximately 40 feet above the ground. Follow the chimney to the tree ledge on the Escalator. The route can be completed in one long or two short pitches.

81. THE SHADOW   Class 5.8

FA: February 1968; C. Raymond

Seventy-five feet right of the base of the Escalator a thin
flake leads up 35 feet to a smooth steep shallow groove
about ten feet in length. Ascend to the groove via a difficult
lieback and easier face climbing. After ascending the
groove, continue up and right on easy ledges to the Escalator.

82. FREE LANCE   Class 5.10

FA: November 1971; J. Long, B. Pottorff.

Ascend the initial lieback of the Shadow for 15 feet. Move
right on a difficult mantle and traverse to a bolt. Easier face
climbing leads up and right to a series of three bolts. The
climbing past the bolts is both strenuous and delicate. The
third bolt protects a difficult traverse right six feet to a sloping platform. From the platform a vegetated crack system
leads right to a chimney and easier climbing. A more challenging finish is to climb a groove or thin crack straight up
about 40 feet (the first 20 feet are 5.10) to the ledge of the
Escalator.

83. AXE OF GOD   Class 5.8

FA: May 1968; L. Harrell, P. Callis

One hundred feet to the right of the beginning of the Escalator, two massive guillotine-like flakes have fallen and

now lean ominously against the base of the wall. From the top of these flakes one may climb with some difficulty into a right curving arch. From the bottom of the arch there appear to be several possible alternatives, but only the one which stays in the arch has been ascended. As the arch starts to curve right the moves are tricky and protection is meager. The leader may place better protection by climbing momentarily out of the crack on the left before committing himself to the arch. Several feet after the arch has bent over horizontally, exit vertically on large holds to a ledge which connects with the Escalator.

84. BS ARCH   Class 5.9

FA: August 1973; J. Smith, T. Burns.

From the top of the fallen flake just right of the Axe of God, climb the small face to the undercling lieback which is followed for about 80 feet. Near the end of the crack move onto the face above. Continue up and left 50 feet to a steep headwall which is ascended directly.

85. FLATMAN CHIMNEY   Class 5.9

FA: May 1968; P. Callis, L. Harrell

About 50 feet right of the Axe of God is a deep cavernous crack. From the cave at its base one is tempted to stay inside and try to squeeze through a narrow part into the wider section above. Several climbers have tried this without success; it is very tight. The alternative is a strenuous move on the outside. Once over the bulge and into the wider fissure above, the climbing is very easy. The pitch ends at the Escalator.

86. GODZILLA'S RETURN   Class 5.10+

FA: April 1972; J. Long, H. Aprin

This severe route starts on the smooth face directly above Flat Man's Chimney and can be easily reached by climbing the first portion of the Escalator. Very difficult face climbing leads past three bolts to a belay alcove beneath the headwall. A difficult mantle of the "Toad's Lip" leads to a bolt which protects the next 30 feet, the crux of the climb. For adequate safety, another bolt is desirable on this lead. A short tricky traverse left is followed by a series of strenuous moves on rounded knobs to a fifth bolt. Difficult 5.9 edging continues 30 feet to a belay ledge. An easy crack leads off of the route to the left, but another fine pitch is found above for those wanting a longer climb. From the right end of the belay ledge, 5.9 moves lead past two bolts. Above delightful 5.8 friction leads to the top.

VARIATION—MONTEZUMA'S REVENGE   Class 5.9

This variation on the Godzilla face is due to T. Sorenson, G. Lewis and J. Wilson. From the right margin of the Godzilla face, traverse up and left a few feet to ascend the slanting lieback which breaks the overhang at this point. Undercling left and then continue straight up 100 feet to a belay ledge just below a second overhang. Mantle the overhang, traverse right to a bolt and continue up to the top.

183

87. HAIR-PIE   Class 5.9

FA: August 1973; T. Burns, L. Swearingen

The face between Flatman Chimney and Hair Lip was long
a candidate for a new route. The present version starts
from the first bolt on Hair Lip. Traverse left to a small foothold then up with difficult edging to larger solution depressions. Follow obvious cracks to easier rock, ending the route
with an enjoyable jam crack.

88. HAIR LIP   Class 5.10

FA: October 1970; I. Couch, L. Reynolds

Hair Lip is an exciting climb on the lip or edge above the
right-facing chimney of Hot Buttered Rump. A thin crack
on the face between Flatman Chimney and Hot Buttered
Rump is ascended to a point ten feet below its end. Climb
up and right (5.8) to a bolt on the corner above Hot Buttered Rump. Follow the "lip" 100 feet to its end. A second
bolt gives good protection for a peculiar 5.10 move leading
to relatively easier climbing.

89. HOT BUTTERED RUMP   Class 5.10

FA: April 1968; C. Raymond, L. Harrell

There are two spectacular flaring chimneys in the Northern
Area of Suicide Rock. The first is a right-facing, slightly
overhanging chimney about 30 feet to the right of Flatman
Chimney. The route ascends this in one pitch of challeng-

ing climbing. The difficulty of placing sound protection adds to the insecurity felt in this strongly flared chimney.

90. SIDE SHOW   Class 5.9

FA: I. Couch, M. Dent

Ascend the face just right of Hot Buttered Rump. Two bolts protect interesting face climbing leading to a long sloping ramp, which in turn leads to North Gully East.

THE NORTHERN AREA
EAGLE PINNACLE GROUP

ROUTES 91–97

The central feature of the Northern Area is Eagle Pinnacle, a prominent pinnacle with a spectacular northeast face. I have heard several stories about how this name was attached to the pinnacle, and since I'm the one who named it, I can assure you that they are all false. It derived its name simply from the existence of the old hawk's or eagle's nest on a ledge high on the north side. The pinnacle is flanked on the two sides by easy 5th class gullies. From high up in either gully it is an easy matter to reach the notch behind the pinnacle from which 30 feet of easy scrambling leads to the top of the pinnacle. Two routes are found on the front face: Small Affair on the left, and Eagle's Nest on the right.

91. NORTH GULLY EAST   Class 5.0

FA: Unknown

An obvious wide gully cleaves the North Face to the left of Eagle Pinnacle. Most of the gully is pleasant 4th class scrambling, but many climbers will want a chock at a point about midway up the gully.

92. QUESTION OF BALANCE   Class 5.10+

FA: July 1973; T. Sorenson, B. Antel

Two spectacular face routes are found on the small face near the top of the rock between North Gully East and Eagle Pinnacle. This face may be reached by ascending either this gully or the Escalator (Route 78) to its end. Question of Balance starts near the left edge of this face. Follow a hairline crack up and left, exiting right (5.10) as soon as possible. Ascend 20 feet to a bolt. Above a few 5.8 moves and easier climbing lead to the summit. Although some nuts can be used in the cracks, several horizontal or knifeblade pitons are required for adequate protection.

93. JIGSAW   Class 5.9

FA: July 1973; T. Sorenson, B. Antel, J. Long, R. Muir,
      R. Harrison, B. Foster.

Near the right edge of the face described above, jam a thin crack or lieback a flake to a small stance. Face climbing leads 15 feet to a bolt which protects the most difficult climbing on the steeper face above. This pitch requires no pitons; it can be adequately protected by the one bolt and seven or eight chocks.

94. SMALL AFFAIR   Class 5.9

FA: 1977; J. Long, W. Antel

From the base of the previous two routes, the upper east face of Eagle Pinnacle is easily reached. The route ascends to a bolt and then traverses right to an edge and up to the summit.

95. RAZOR'S EDGE   Class 5.8

FA: J. Wilson, T. Sorenson, J. Long.

The north side of Eagle Pinnacle has as its main feature a broad triangular bowl. Prominent cracks on the two margins meet at the apex. Neither of these crack systems has yet been climbed. Just right of center is a large flake extending about halfway up the bowl. The left edge of this flake is the Razor's Edge and leads to the main right crack about halfway up. Continue to the apex of the bowl where rappel rings will be found. It is reported possible to continue up the vertical grungy dihedral above, but it is very unpleasant climbing.

For whatever it is worth, the flake houses a large number of bats. I doubt that this poses a hazard to the climber, but bat bites are not to be treated lightly.

96. EAGLE'S NEST   Class 5.9

FA: June 1970; C. & E. Wilts

The Eagle's Nest is found on the northwest buttress of the face of Eagle Pinnacle. On the first ascent, the middle of the face was climbed 100 feet to a broad bowl. From the center of the bowl climb right and up to an excellent belay ledge. Here ascend a short but difficult overhanging chimney to the buttress ridge on the right. Another 50 feet of pleasant climbing leads unexpectedly to an old nest of an eagle or hawk—an excellent belay spot well hidden from view. Climbers are urged to avoid damaging the old nest. Above, easier 4th class climbing leads to the top of the pinnacle.

The easiest route of descent involves a short 4th class crack on the back side to the notch behind the pinnacle. From here it is easiest to traverse right to North Gully West and climb or rappel to the bottom. The first free ascent of the overhanging chimney was made by T. Sorenson, M. Graham and W. Antel.

97. NORTH GULLY WEST   Class 5.4

FA: Unknown

A second obvious gully is found on the right side of Eagle Pinnacle. The most difficult move is found just below the top. This route is a good rappel route since several trees are found in the gully for rappel anchors. This gully also provides the easiest route of ascent of Eagle Pinnacle.

THE NORTHERN AREA
CAT'S CAVE INN
AND ENVIRONS

ROUTES 98–114

Beyond the Eagle Pinnacle area, the face of Suicide Rock is smaller in vertical height, but a marvelous variety of problems are found in the closely spaced routes between Eagle Pinnacle and the end of the rock.

98. FLAKES OF WRATH   Class 5.10+

FA: 1975; Bachar and others (Lewis, Wilson, Long, Eriksson, Sorenson)

Between North Gully West and Cat's Cave Inn, the small face is broken by one crack system. Ascend a thin lieback, traverse slightly left and continue up the crack to the belay stance of Flakeout. The second pitch is slightly easier. Continue straight up on some loose flakes (5.9) to a bolt and easier 5.8 climbing to the top.

99. FLAKE-OUT   Class 5.7

FA: September 1967; P. Callis, C. Raymond, P. Raymond

This climb angles left across the face just left of the large
right-facing dihedral of the Cat's Cave Inn. Start at the base
of the dihedral. Climb 30 feet up the corner on the left on
easy rock and traverse 20 feet left on a narrow ledge. Climb
up ten feet and diagonal left 20 feet on broken rock to the
right edge of a prominent flake. Somewhat strenuous
climbing leads to a belay position at the top of the flake. On
the second pitch, traverse left around or over another flake
and continue left to the base of a shallow trough. Ascend
the trough by lieback and stemming to the top.

100. SPOOKY SPIKE   Class 5.8

FA: December 1968; C. Raymond, W. Burke, P. Raymond

Ascend to the narrow ledge of Flake-Out. After the short
lieback above, continue straight up to a steep right-facing
dihedral. A delicate step allows one to reach a crack on the
left wall of the dihedral, which is ascended to a narrow
ledge. From the left end of this ledge climb upward and
slightly to the right to a left-facing dihedral containing a de-
licately perched 15-foot high blade of rock. In climbing the
dihedral, the tempting holds offered by this flake must be
considered strictly off route.

101. ETUDE   Class 5.8 & A2 or 5.11

FA: September 1969; L. Reynolds, R. Wendell

On the face of the buttress just left of Cat's Cave Inn and just right of the Flake Out there are four roughly parallel closely spaced cracks. Three of these peter out part way up the face, but the second from the right continues up about 100 feet to an overhanging but more broken area. On early ascents, this crack was climbed with direct aid using tied-off pitons in a bottoming crack. On the second pitch, direct aid pitons behind a hollow column led to easier (5.5) free climbing up and right to the top of the rock. The first free ascent was made by J. Long, R. Accomazzo, R. Harrison and T. Sorenson. The most difficult climbing is near the end of the first pitch. The second pitch is about 5.8 in difficulty. Nut placement is difficult, and provides at best rather inadequate protection.

102. FLOWER OF HIGH RANK   Class 5.9

FA: October 1972; R. Muir, M. Graham

Between Etude and Cat's Cave Inn, a narrow finger or jam crack leads to a solitary pine tree about 100 feet above the ground. Above the pine tree go right around a corner and up to a ceiling. Exit left and ascend 20 feet to a belay stance. Continue up to join Etude 15 feet from the top. This spectacular climb is well protected by chocks.

An alternative ending (Crysanthemum variation) is equally difficult. From the lone pine, traverse left and lieback up to the usual belay stance of Etude.

A more challenging ending (5.10+) exits right along an overhanging dihedral. This variation called Wet Dreams is due to T. Sorenson.

103. CAT'S CAVE INN   Class 5.8

FA: September 1968; C. Raymond, P. Callis

Near the north end of the rock, where the wall begins curving around to the west, there is a giant right-facing dihedral containing a chimney. This route ascends the chimney and dihedral above. The first pitch involves no major difficulties; belay on top of a large flake in the chimney. The second pitch involves somewhat strenuous jamming. The final pitch is ascended by staying left in the right angle corner of the dihedral. It is difficult to get started, but the improbable looking overhang above is turned with relative ease.

104. YOURS   Class 5.7

FA: March 1972; P. White, L. Reynolds, D. Gilbert

Between Cat's Cave Inn and Graham Crackers the face is broken by two close lines of weakness consisting of flake systems and jam cracks. There are several interconnecting ledges where one can cross from one to the other. These can be combined in a variety of ways to give a nice two- or three-pitch route ranging from 5.7 to 5.8 in difficulty.

Rather than indicate the two or three specific routes furnished by various climbers, it seems more appropriate here to let the climber work out his own combination. All routes reported can be protected by nuts if one carries a full range of sizes from small stoppers to #8 hex.

105. GRAHAM CRACKERS   Class 5.6

FA: April 1968; D. Lashier, P. Raymond

Thirty feet to the right of Cat's Cave Inn and immediately above a small sugar pine is an obvious break in the sloping Northeast Face. Graham Crackers follows this break. Two pitches of enjoyable climbing lead to the summit. The main difficulty is a smooth trough high on the face. After ascending this trough, climb up to the left side of a prominent downpointing horn, then climb back to the right onto its crest. Scrambling brings one to the top.

106. THE GUILLOTINE   Class 5.8

FA: October 1969; A. Steck, C. Wilts

The route starts at a medium-sized fir tree about 25 feet right of Graham Crackers. Climb to the top of a large fallen flake at the base of the rock. First a small flake and then a large flake, the Guillotine, are passed using an improbable looking but surprisingly easy lieback. From the top of the Guillotine continue up the main crack ten feet. Turn an awkward corner on the right and lieback up ten feet to enter a narrow ten-foot chimney that cannot be seen from below. Exit at the top of the chimney on small lieback flakes on the main face. Where these end under a slight overhang, climb up and slightly left to a good belay ledge. A second pitch of interesting but easy friction ends the climb.

107. THE SUPERFLUOUS BOLT   Class 5.9

FA: I. Couch, M. Cohen, M. Dent

Immediately right of the Guillotine a steep shallow dihedral can be seen beginning 50 feet above the ground. To reach the dihedral, climb. the face past a small overhang and a bolt. Continue up the dihedral to the top of the wall.

108. OBSCURED BY CLOUDS   Class 5.10

FA: M. Graham, T. Sorenson, G. Lewis

An interesting face route is found between the Superfluous Bolt and Harm's Way. The hardest moves are found passing the second of two small overhangs and face climbing above to a bolt belay. The second pitch is slightly easier (5.9) and ascends the face directly, about 75 feet left of the upper part of Harm's Way. This route is adequately protected by an assortment of stoppers.

109. HARM'S WAY   Class 5.10+

FA: October 1970; I. Couch, M. Dent, L. Reynolds

Twenty feet right of the Guillotine a flake system leads up to a dike leading right and up. From the end of the dike climb up and right to a ledge which is only ten feet left of Tabby Treat. A bolt here can be used to anchor the belay. From the extreme lower left end of the ledge, continuous 5.9 face climbing leads past the bolt to a very thin crack where several very poor tied-off pitons may be placed to protect very difficult (5.10) climbing leading up and left to an overhang. Don't worry, the overhang is easily passed if reached.

From the belay ledge it is a simple matter to traverse to Tabby Treat. This provides an interesting two pitch climb that does not exceed 5.6 in difficulty.

110. TABBY TREAT   Class 5.1

FA: May 1968; C. Raymond, P. Raymond

At the right margin of the broad face to the right of Cat's Cave Inn is an obvious left-facing dihedral. The route ascends a shallow broad gully and continues up the dihedral in two pitches of easy climbing on slightly crumbly rock.

111. THE THIN MAN   Class 5.9

FA: H. Chuntz, R. Coplin

Midway between Tabby Treat and Breakout, several thin cracks zigzag up the face toward two overhangs. A bolt protects delicate moves near the beginning. Exit left under the larger overhang to a belay ledge. Easy friction ends the climb.

112. BREAK OUT   Class 5.6

FA: October 1970; L. Reynolds, H. Aprin

From a point 50 feet right of Tabby Treat a large orange scar is visible about 40 feet from the ground. Climb the face below to a small ledge. From this ledge ascend a short jam crack to the orange scar. Continue up and left to the skyline above the Tabby Treat dihedral. Enjoyable face climbing leads to a belay ledge.

113. LITTLE MURDERS   Class 5.2

FA: March 1972; A. Vick, S. Mackey

Start in the right-facing open book about 60 feet right of Tabby Treat. Lieback, jam and finally chimney up the dihedral until one can exit left on good holds. Continue to a ledge about 50 feet above the ground. Above, about 40 feet of 4th class scrambling leads to the top. A traverse left to the upper pitch of Break Out provides a more interesting finish.

114. INNOMINATE II   Class 5.8

FA: Unknown

Little Murders is at the left margin of a small rock face, the last significant rock exposure at the north end of Suicide Rock. A one-pitch zigzag route leads up this face, staying generally near the center. Near the top, a piton can be placed in a small left-facing crack to protect the most difficult move above and to the left.

WESTERN AZALEA
Rhododendron occidentale

INDEX
TO
ROUTES

TAHQUITZ ROCK

	ROUTE	CLASSIFICATION	ROUTE NO.
A	Angel's Fright	5.4	39
	Angle Iron Traverse	5.7	48
B	Baby's Butt	5.5	74
	Bat	5.10+	25
	Big Daddy	5.10	81
	Black Harlot's Layaway	5.11	66
	Blank	5.10	35
	Blanketty Blank	5.10	43
C	Chauvinist	5.7	61
	Chingadera	5.11	65
	Chin Strap Crack	5.10	26
	Climb With No Beginning	5.6	75
	Consolation	5.9	15
D	Daley's Direct	5.6	72
	Dave's Deviation	5.10	33
	Devil's Delight	5.9	34
	Diddly	5.10	76
E	El Camino Real	5.10	49
	El Dorado	5.9	4
	El Grandote	5.9	4
	El Whampo	5.7	3
	Error	5.6	10
F	Fingergrip	5.7	47
	Fingertip Traverse	5.3	46
	Fingertrip	5.7	45
	Fitschen's Folly	5.6	78
	Flakes	5.11	24
	Flying Circus	5.11 & A4	58
	Fool's Rush	5.6	20
	Frightful Fright	5.11	40

TAHQUITZ ROCK

ROUTE	CLASSIFICATION	ROUTE NO.
Frightful Variation of The Trough	5.2	37
Friction Route	3	79
From Bad Traverse	4	28
G Gallwas Gallop	5.9	31
Grace Slick	5.10	5
Grandote	5.9	4
Green Arch	5.11	57
Gulp	5.9	14
H Hangover	5.12	50
Hard Lark	5.7	7
Hoodenett	5.9	13
Hubris	5.10	8
Human Fright	5.10	41
I Illegitimate	5.9	18
Innominate	5.9	68
J Jam Crack	5.7	33
Jensen's Jaunt	5.6	51
Jonah	5.10+	36
L Lark	5.3	7
Last Judgement	5.11	53
Le Toit	5.11	22
Little Momma	5.10	82
Lizard's Leap	5.9	77
Long Climb	5.7	17
M Magical Mystery Tour	5.11	12
Mechanic's Route	5.8	56
N North Buttress	5.3	9
Northeast Face	5.6	5
Northeast Farce	5.4	3
Northeast Rib	5.0	2
Notches	2 to 3	1
0 Offshoot	5.8	60

ROUTE	CLASSIFICATION	ROUTE NO.
Open Book	5.9	54
Orange Peel	5.5	73
P Pas de Deux	5.10	71
Passover	5.10	27
Pearly Gate	5.9	53
Piton Pooper	5.7	30
R Rack	5.9	32
Reach	5.11	67
Red Rock Route	5.1	80
Right Ski Track	5.8	64
Royal's Arches—Lower	5.10+	29
Royal's Arches—Upper	5.7	29
S Sahara Terror	5.6	11
Sham	5.10 & A2	16
Ski Tracks	5.5	63
Slab	5.8	44
Sling Swing Traverse	5.9	62
Stairway to Heaven	5.9 & A4	24
Step	5.9	21
Super Pooper	5.9	23
Swallow	5.8	14
Swing Traverse	5.1	38
Switchbacks	5.8	42
T Tahquitz Rock Summit	2 & 3	1
TM's Jewel	5.7 & A4	70
Toe Bias	5.9	6
Toe Tip	5.8	45
Traitor Horn	5.8	52
Trough	5.0	32
U Unchaste	5.10+	59
Uneventful	5.5	8
Upside Down Cake	5.10	83
V Vampire	5.10+	25

TAHQUITZ ROCK

ROUTE	CLASSIFICATION	ROUTE NO.
W West Lark	5.5	7
White Maiden's Walkaway	5.1	19
Wong Climb	5.8	17
X X-Crack	5.7 & A4	69
Z Ziggy Stardust	5.10+	27
Zigzag	5.10	55

SUICIDE ROCK

	ROUTE	CLASSIFICATION	ROUTE NO.
A	Arpa Carpa	5.9	1
	Arsy Farcy	5.10	55
	Axe of God	5.8	83
B	BC's Ouch Chimney	5.9	29
	Blown Out	5.10+	17
	Bolts to Nowhere	5.11	11
	Break Out	5.6	112
	Breeze	5.8	80
	BS Arch	5.9	84
	Buttress Chimney	5.6	42
	Bye Gully	5.5	61
C	Cat's Cave Inn	5.8	103
	Captain Hook	5.7	51
	Chatsworth Chimney	5.5	20
	Chisholm Trail	5.11	28
	Clam Chowder	5.8	66
	Commencement	5.9	65
	Continuation	5.6	64
D	David	5.7	73
	Deception Pillar	5.9	8
	Delila	5.8	75
	Dilemma	A3	77
	Double Exposure	5.11	49
	Down and Out	5.10	18
	Drain Pipe	5.11	34
	Drowned Out	5.9	19
E	Eagle's Nest	5.9	96
	East Buttress Gully	5.2	56
	Escalator	5.6	78
	Euphoria	5.6 & A2	32
	Etude	5.11	101

SUICIDE ROCK

	ROUTE	CLASSIFICATION	ROUTE NO.
F	Fiend	5.9	21
	Flake-Out	5.7	99
	Flakes of Wrath	5.10+	98
	Flatman Chimney	5.9	85
	Flower of High Rank	5.9	102
	Forest Lawn	A2	4
	Free Lance	5.10	82
	Frustration	5.10	53
G	Garbage Gulch	5.1	26
	Gates of Delirium	5.11	33
	Godzilla's Return	5.10+	86
	Goliath	5.7	72
	Graham Crackers	5.6	105
	Guillotine	5.8	106
H	Hair Lip	5.10	88
	Hair-pie	5.9	87
	Harm's Way	5.10+	109
	Hernia	5.8	55
	Hesitation	5.10	40
	Hot Buttered Rump	5.10	89
I	Innominate II	5.8	114
	Insomnia	5.11	48
	Iron Cross	5.10+	36
J	Jackal	5.9	79
	Jammit	5.9	7
	Jigsaw	5.9	93
L	Last Dance	5.10	16
	Le Dent	5.6	6
	Limp Dick	5.10	15
	Little Murders	5.2	113
	Low Pressure	5.10	59
M	Major	5.7	14
	Mantle of No Return	5.9	46
	Man Who Fell to Earth	5.10+	30

SUICIDE ROCK

ROUTE	CLASSIFICATION	ROUTE NO.
Mickey Mantle	5.8	22
Minor	5.1	14
Miscalculation	5.10+	12
Mogen David	5.8	73
Montezuma's Revenge	5.9	86
Munge Dihedral	5.9	3
Mushy Peach	5.10	62
N New Generation	5.11	39
North Gully East	5.0	91
North Gully West	5.4	97
O Obscured by Clouds	5.10	108
Ouch Chimney	5.9	29
P Paisano Chimney	5.8	31
Paisano Jam Crack	5.9	45
Paisano Overhang	5.12	44
Pass Time	5.9	52
Pink Royd	5.10+	24
Pirate	5.12	50
Plague	5.7	57
Q Question of Balance	5.10+	92
Quiet Desperation	5.11	35
R Razor's Edge	5.8	95
Rebolting Development	5.10+	74
Revelation	5.9	68
Root Canal	5.7	5
S Sampson	5.9	71
Season's End	5.11	76
Sensuous Corner	5.9	25
Serpentine	5.9	69
Shadow	5.8	81
Short Story	5.6	9
Side Show	5.9	90
Skigliack	5.9	63
Small Affair	5.9	94

SUICIDE ROCK

ROUTE	CLASSIFICATION	ROUTE NO.
Source	5.10	27
Spooky Spike	5.8	100
Spring Cleaning	5.6	13
Step Away	5.7	43
Stretch	5.9	41
Sundance	5.10	37
Superfluous Bolt	5.9	107
Superfly	–	47
Surprise	5.8	67
Sword of Damocles	5.9	54
T Tabby Treat	5.1	110
Ten Carat Gold	5.10	70
Thin Man	5.9	111
Twilight Delight	5.9	10
U Ultimatum	5.10	23
V Valhalla	5.11	38
Voodoo Child	5.11	40
W Warm Up	5.8	60
Wet Dreams	5.10+	102
Wild Gazongas	5.10	2
Y Yours	5.7	104
Z Zucchinis from Alpha Centauri	5.10	58